AF609482

ASSAM

A STATE STUDY GUIDE

PIYUSH GOGOI

HAWK PRESS

Published by

Hawk Press
4836/24, Ansari Road, Daryaganj
New Delhi – 110 002
Phones: 91-11-23278618, 91-11-43667199
E-mail: thehawkpress@gmail.com
www.thehawkpress.com

ISBN: 978-93-88318-87-7

Preface

Assam is a state in Northeast India, situated south of the eastern Himalayas along the Brahmaputra and Barak River valleys. Assam covers an area of 78,438 km (30,285 sq mi). The state is bordered by Bhutan and the state of Arunachal Pradesh to the north; Nagaland and Manipur to the east; Meghalaya, Tripura, Mizoram and Bangladesh to the south; and West Bengal to the west via the Siliguri Corridor, a 22 kilometres (14 mi) strip of land that connects the state to the rest of India.

Prosperous in the historical, cultural and religious domain, the state, conceivably is unrivalled in its vicissitude. Perhaps, several volumes can be inscribed even if a single aspect of Assam, full of mountains, plateaus, rivers-streams, various tribal, dense forests and rare wild species, is touched upon.

The indigenous people traditionally include ethnic groups like Assamese Brahmins (including Ganaks), Koch Rajbongshi, Ahom, Bodo, Mishings, Sonowal Kacharis, Rabha, Hajong , Karbi, Kuki , Meitei people, Rengma Naga, Chutias, Kalitas, Keot (Kaibarta), Tiwa, Mech Kachari,Hmar, Thengal-Kacharis, Sarania Kacharis, Dimasa, Tea Tribes, Tai Phake and other Tai groups, indigenous ethnic groups of other neighbouring North-East states, Deoris, Doms/Nadiyals, Assamese Muslims (particularly Goria, Moria, Deshi communities), Assamese Sikhs and Assamese Christians speaking Assamese or any other tribal dialect of Assam as their mother tongue.

The political structure of Assam in India is headed by the ceremonial post of the Governor. He is assisted by a council of ministers, headed by the Chief Minister, who are members of the Assam Assembly. In recent years the Governor has become more powerful, especially because the last two Governors have been ex-Army generals and the Army is entrusted with anti-insurgency operations against ULFA and other armed groups.

Assam isn't just a part of India's enigmatic orient; it is a microcosm of the country. There isn't a single sub-continental community--from a village (Kampur) of localized Sikhs to Tamils in the vicinity of Guwahati's Balaji Temple and Afghans -- that hasn't settled down across the 78,438 sq km area the state occupies. No wonder, Assam has four official languages -- Assamese, Bengali, Bodo and English -- and publishes school textbooks in 14, almost equal to the number of primary tongues recognized by the Constitution of India.

Assamese and Bodo are the major indigenous and official languages of the state while Bengali holds official status in particular districts in the Barak Valley. Traditionally Assamese was the language of the commons (of mixed origin - Bodo, Khasi, Sanskrit, Magadhan Prakrit) of the ancient kingdoms such as Kamrupa and Kamatapur in Assam.

This is a reference book. All the matter is just compiled and edited in nature, taken from the various sources which are in public domain.

The book is an asset for all scholars, researchers, teachers, students and ofcourse, the general readers.

—Editor

ABOUT THE BOOK

Assam is a state in Northeast India, situated south of the eastern Himalayas along the Brahmaputra and Barak River valleys. Assam covers an area of 78,438 km (30,285 sq mi). The state is bordered by Bhutan and the state of Arunachal Pradesh to the north; Nagaland and Manipur to the east; Meghalaya, Tripura, Mizoram and Bangladesh to the south; and West Bengal to the west via the Siliguri Corridor, a 22 kilometres (14 mi) strip of land that connects the state to the rest of India. Assam is in many ways a country of exceptional interest. Hemmed in as India is, by the sea on the South-east and South-west, and by the lofty chain of the Himalayas on the North, the only routes between it and the rest of Asia which are practicable for migration on a large scale, lie on its North-West and North-east confines, the so-called Aryans, and many later invaders, such as the Greeks, the Huns, the Pathans, and the Mughals, entered India from the North-west from the North-east, through Assam have come successive hordes of immigrants from the great hive of the Mongolian race in Western China. Assam has Governor Jagdish Mukhi as the head of the state, the unicameral Assam Legislative Assembly of 126 members, and a government led by the Chief Minister of Assam. The state is divided into five regional divisions. The book is an asset for all scholars, researchers, teachers, students and ofcourse, the general readers.

Contents

1

State at a Glance

Assam is a state in Northeast India, situated south of the eastern Himalayas along the Brahmaputra and Barak River valleys. Assam covers an area of 78,438 km (30,285 sq mi). The state is bordered by Bhutan and the state of Arunachal Pradesh to the north; Nagaland and Manipur to the east; Meghalaya, Tripura, Mizoram and Bangladesh to the south; and West Bengal to the west via the Siliguri Corridor, a 22 kilometres (14 mi) strip of land that connects the state to the rest of India.

The indigenous people traditionally include ethnic groups like Assamese Brahmins (including Ganaks), Koch Rajbongshi, Ahom, Bodo, Mishings, Sonowal Kacharis, Rabha, Hajong , Karbi, Kuki , Meitei people, Rengma Naga, Chutias, Kalitas, Keot (Kaibarta), Tiwa, Mech Kachari,Hmar, Thengal-Kacharis, Sarania Kacharis, Dimasa, Tea Tribes, Tai Phake and other Tai groups, indigenous ethnic groups of other neighbouring North-East states, Deoris, Doms/Nadiyals, Assamese Muslims (particularly Goria, Moria, Deshi communities), Assamese Sikhs and Assamese Christians speaking Assamese or any other tribal dialect of Assam as their mother tongue.

Assam is known for Assam tea and Assam silk. The state has conserved the one-horned Indian rhinoceros from near extinction, along with the wild water buffalo, pygmy hog, tiger and various species of Asiatic birds, and provides one of the last wild habitats for the Asian elephant. The Assamese economy is aided by wildlife tourism to Kaziranga National Park and Manas National Park, which are World Heritage Sites. Sal tree forests are found in the state which, as a result of abundant rainfall, look green all year round. Assam receives more rainfall than most parts of India; this rain feeds the Brahmaputra River, whose tributaries and oxbow lakesprovide the region with a hydro-geomorphic environment.

Etymology

The precise etymology of modern anglicised word "Assam" is ambiguous. In the classical period and up to the 12th century the region east of the Karatoya river, largely congruent to present-day Assam, was called Kamarupa, and alternatively, Pragjyotisha.In medieval times the Mughals used *Asham* (eastern Assam) and Kamrup (western Assam), and during British colonialism, the English used Assam. Though many authors have associated the name with the 13th century Shan invaders the precise origin of the name is not clear. It was suggested by some that the Sanskrit word *Asama* ("unequalled", "peerless", etc.) was the root, which has been rejected by Kakati, and more recent authors have concurred that it is a latter-day Sanskritization of a native name.Among possible origins are Tai (*A-Cham*) and Bodo (*Ha-Sam*).

HISTORY

Pre-history

Assam and adjoining regions have evidences of human settlements from all the periods of the Stone ages. The hills at the height of 1,500–2,000 feet (460 to 615 m) were popular habitats probably due to availability of exposed dolerite basalt, useful for tool-making.

Legendary

According to a late text, Kalika Purana (c. 9th–10th century AD), the earliest ruler of Assam was Mahiranga Danav of the Danava dynasty, which was removed by Naraka who established the Naraka dynasty. The last of these rulers, also Naraka, was slain by Krishna. Naraka's son Bhagadatta became the king, who (it is mentioned in the Mahabharata) fought for the Kauravas in the battle of Kurukshetra with an army of *kiratas*, *chinas* and *dwellers of the eastern coast*. At the same time towards east in central Assam, Asura Kingdom was ruled by indigenous line of kings of Mariachi dynasty.

Ancient

Samudragupta's 4th century Allahabad pillar inscription mentions Kamarupa (Western Assam) and Davaka (Central Assam) as frontier kingdoms of the Gupta Empire.

Davaka was later absorbed by Kamarupa, which grew into a large kingdom that spanned from Karatoya river to near present Sadiyaand covered the entire Brahmaputra valley, North Bengal, parts of Bangladesh and, at times Purnea and parts of West Bengal.

The kingdom was ruled by three dynasties; the Varmanas (c. 350–650 CE), the Mlechchha dynasty (c.655–900 CE) and the Kamarupa-Palas (c. 900–1100 CE), from their capitals in present-day Guwahati (Pragjyotishpura), Tezpur (Haruppeswara) and North Gauhati(Durjaya) respectively. All three dynasties claimed descent from Narakasura.

In the reign of the Varman king, Bhaskaravarman (c. 600–650 AD), the Chinese traveller Xuanzang visited the region and recorded his travels. Later, after weakening and disintegration (after the Kamarupa-Palas), the Kamarupa tradition was extended to c. 1255 AD by the Lunar I (c. 1120–1185 AD) and Lunar II (c. 1155–1255 AD) dynasties.

Medieval

Three later dynasties were the Ahoms, the Chutiya and the Koch.

The Ahoms, a Tai group, ruled Upper Assam The Shans built their kingdom and consolidated their power in Eastern Assam with the modern town of Sibsagar as their capital. Until the early 1500s, the Ahoms ruled a small kingdom in Sibsagar district and suddenly expanded during King Suhungmung's rule taking advantage of weakening rule of Chutia and Dimasa kingdoms. By 1681, the whole tract down to the border of the modern district of Goalpara came permanently under their sway. Ahoms ruled for nearly 600 years (1228–1826 AD) with major expansions in the early 16th century at the cost of Chutia and Dimasa Kacharikingdoms. Since c. the 13th century AD, the nerve centre of Ahom polity was upper Assam; the kingdom was gradually extended to the Karatoya River in the 17th or 18th century. It was at its zenith during the reign of Sukhrungphaa or Sworgodeu Rudra Sinha (c. 1696–1714 AD).

The Chutiya rulers (1187–1673 AD), a Bodo-Kachari group by origin, held the regions on both the banks of Brahmaputra with its domain in the area eastwards from Vishwanath (north bank) and Buridihing (south bank), in Upper Assam and in the state of Arunachal Pradesh. It was partially annexed in the early 1500s by the Ahoms, finally getting absorbed in 1673 AD. The rivalry between the Chutiyas and Ahoms for the supremacy of eastern Assam led to a series of battles between them from the early 16th century until the start of the 17th century, which saw great loss of men and money.

The Koch, another Bodo-Kachari dynasty, established sovereignty in c. 1510 AD. The Koch kingdom in Western Assam and present North Bengal was at its zenith in the early reign of Nara Narayan (c. 1540–1587 AD). It split into two in c. 1581 AD, the western part as a Moghul vassal and the eastern as an Ahom satellite state. Later, in 1682, Koch Hajo was entirely annexed by the Ahoms.

Among other dynasties, the Dimasa Kacharis (13th century-1854 AD) ruled from Dikhow River to central and southern Assam and had their capital at Dimapur. With expansion of Ahom kingdom, by the early 17th century, the Chutiya areas were annexed and since c. 1536 AD the Kacharis remained only in Cachar and North Cachar, and more as an Ahom ally than a competing force.

Despite numerous invasions, mostly by the Muslim rulers, no western power ruled Assam until the arrival of the British. Though the Mughals made seventeen attempts to invade, they were never successful. The most successful invader Mir Jumla, a governor of Aurangzeb, briefly occupied Garhgaon (c. 1662–63 AD), the then capital, but found it difficult to prevent guerrilla attacks on his forces, forcing them to leave. The decisive victory of the Assamese led by general Lachit Borphukan on the Mughals, then under command of Raja Ram Singha, at Saraighat in 1671 almost ended Mughal ambitions in this region. The Mughals were finally expelled from Lower Assam during the reign of Gadadhar Singha in 1682 AD.

Colonial era

The discovery of *Camellia sinensis* in 1834 in Assam was followed by testing in 1836–37 in London. The British allowed companies to rent land from 1839 onwards. Thereafter tea plantations mushroomed in Eastern Assam, where the soil and the climate were most suitable.

Problems with the imported labourers from China and hostility from native Assamese resulted in the migration of forced labourers from central and eastern parts of India. After initial trial and error with planting the Chinese and the Assamese-Chinese hybrid varieties, the planters later accepted the local *Camellia assamica* as the most suitable variety for Assam. By the 1850s, the industry started seeing some profits. The industry saw initial growth, when in 1861, investors were allowed to own land in Assam and it saw substantial progress with invention of new technologies and machinery for preparing processed tea during the 1870s.

Despite the commercial success, tea labourers continued to be exploited, working and living under poor conditions. Fearful of greater government interference, the tea growers formed the Indian Tea Association in 1888 to lobby to retain the status quo. The organisation was successful in this, but even after India's independence, conditions of the labourers have improved very little.

In the later part of the 18th century, religious tensions and atrocities by the nobles led to the Moamoria rebellion (1769–1805), resulting in tremendous casualties of lives and property. The rebellion was suppressed but the kingdom was severely weakened by the civil war. Political rivalry between Prime Minister Purnananda Burhagohain and Badan Chandra Borphukan, the Ahom Viceroy of Western Assam, led to an invitation to the Burmese by the latter, in turn leading to three successive Burmese invasions of Assam. The reigning monarch Chandrakanta Singha tried to check the Burmese invaders but he was defeated after fierce resistance.

A reign of terror was unleashed by the Burmese on the Assamese people, who fled to neighbouring kingdoms and British-ruled Bengal. The Burmese reached the East India Company's borders, and the First Anglo-Burmese Warensued in 1824. The war ended under the Treaty of Yandabo in 1826, with the Company taking control of Western Assam and installing Purandar Singha as king of Upper Assam in 1833. The arrangement lasted till 1838 and thereafter the British gradually annexed the entire region.

Initially Assam was made a part of the Bengal Presidency, then in 1906 it was made a part of Eastern Bengal and Assamprovince, and in 1912 it was reconstituted into a chief commissioners' province. In 1913, a legislative council and, in 1937, the Assam Legislative Assembly, were formed in Shillong, the erstwhile capital of the region. The British tea planters imported labour from central India adding to the demographic canvas.

The Assam territory was first separated from Bengal in 1874 as the 'North-East Frontier' non-regulation province, also known as the Assam Chief-Commissionership. It was incorporated into the new province of Eastern Bengal and Assam in 1905 after the partition of Bengal (1905–1911) and re-established in 1912 as Assam Province .

After a few initially unsuccessful attempts to gain independence for Assam during the 1850s, anti-colonial

Assamese joined and actively supported the Indian National Congress against the British from the early 20th century, with Gopinath Bordoloi emerging as the preeminent nationalist leader in the Assam Congress. Bordoloi's major political rival in this time was Sir Saidullah, who was representing the Muslim League, and had the backing of the influential Muslim cleric Maulana Bhasani.

The *Assam Postage Circle* was established by 1873 under the headship of the Deputy Post Master General.

At the turn of the 20th century, British India consisted of eight provinces that were administered either by a governor or a lieutenant-governor. Assam Province was one among major eight provinces of British India. The table below shows the major original provinces during British India covering the Assam Province under the Administrative Office of the Chief Commissioner.

With the partition of India in 1947, Assam became a constituent state of India. The Sylhet District of Assam (excluding the Karimganj subdivision) was given up to East Pakistan, which later became Bangladesh.

Modern history

The government of India, which has the unilateral powers to change the borders of a state, divided Assam into several states beginning in 1970 within the borders of what was then Assam. In 1963, the Naga Hills district became the 16th state of India under the name of Nagaland. Part of Tuensang was added to Nagaland. In 1970, in response to the demands of the Khasi, Jaintia and Garo people of the Meghalaya Plateau, the districts embracing the Khasi Hills, Jaintia Hills, and Garo Hills were formed into an autonomous state within Assam; in 1972 this became a separate state under the name of Meghalaya. In 1972, Arunachal Pradesh (the North East Frontier Agency) and Mizoram (from the Mizo Hills in the south) were separated from Assam as union territories; both became states in 1986.

Since the restructuring of Assam after independence, communal tensions and violence remain. Separatist groups began forming along ethnic lines, and demands for autonomy and sovereignty grew, resulting in the fragmentation of Assam. In 1961, the government of Assam passed legislation making use of the Assamese language compulsory. It was withdrawn later under pressure from Bengali speaking people in Cachar. In the 1980s the Brahmaputra valley saw a six-year Assam Agitation triggered by the discovery of a sudden rise in registered voters on electoral rolls. It tried to force the government to identify and deport foreigners illegally migrating from neighbouring Bangladeshand to provide constitutional, legislative, administrative and cultural safeguards for the indigenous Assamese majority, which they felt was under threat due to the increase of migration from Bangladesh. The agitation ended after an accord (Assam Accord 1985) between its leaders and the Union Government, which remained unimplemented, causing simmering discontent.

The post 1970s experienced the growth of armed separatist groups such as the United Liberation Front of Asom (ULFA) and the National Democratic Front of Bodoland (NDFB). In November 1990, the Government of India deployed the Indian army, after which low-intensity military conflicts and political homicides have been continuing for more than a decade. In recent times, ethnically based militant groups have grown. Panchayati Raj Institutions have been applied in Assam, after agitation of the communities due to the sluggish rate of development and general apathy of successive state governments towards Indigenous Assamese communities.

Geography

A significant geographical aspect of Assam is that it contains three of six physiographic divisions of India – The Northern Himalayas (Eastern Hills), The Northern Plains (Brahmaputra plain) and Deccan Plateau (Karbi Anglong). As the Brahmaputra flows in Assam the climate here is cold and there is rainfall most of the month. Geomorphic studies conclude that the Brahmaputra, the life-line of Assam, is an antecedent river older than the Himalayas. The river with steep gorges and rapids in Arunachal Pradesh entering Assam, becomes a braided river (at times 10 mi/16 km wide) and with tributaries, creates a flood plain (Brahmaputra Valley: 50–60 mi/80–100 km wide, 600 mi/1000 km long). The hills of Karbi Anglong, North Cachar and those in and close to Guwahati (also Khasi-Garo Hills) now eroded and dissected are originally parts of the South Indian Plateau system. In the south, the Barak originating in the Barail Range (Assam-Nagaland border) flows through the Cachar district with a 25–30 miles (40–50 km) wide valley and enters Bangladesh with the name Surma River.

Urban Centres include Guwahati, one of the 100 fastest growing cities in the world. Guwahati is the gateway to the North-East India. Silchar, (in the Barak valley) the 2nd most populous city in Assam and an important centre of business, education and tourism. Other large cities include Dibrugarh, an oil, natural gas, tea and tourism industry centre, Jorhat, and Tinsukia.

Climate

With the "Tropical Monsoon Rainforest Climate", Assam is temperate (summer max. at 95–100 °F or 35–38 °C and winter min. at 43–46 °F or 6–8 °C) and experiences heavy rainfall and high humidity. The climate is characterised by heavy monsoon downpours reducing summer temperatures and affecting foggy nights and mornings in winters, frequent during the afternoons. Spring (Mar–Apr) and autumn (Sept–Oct) are usually pleasant with moderate rainfall and temperature. Assam's agriculture usually depends on the south-west monsoon rains.

Flooding

Every year, flooding from the Brahmaputra and other rivers deluges places in Assam. The water levels of the rivers rise because of rainfall resulting in the rivers overflowing their banks and engulfing nearby areas. Apart from houses and livestock being washed away by flood water, bridges, railway tracks and roads are also damaged by the calamity, which causes communication breakdown in many places. Fatalities are also caused by the natural disaster in many places of the State.

Fauna

Assam is one of the richest biodiversity zones in the world and consists of tropical rainforests, deciduous forests, riverine grasslands, bamboo orchards and numerous wetland ecosystems; Many are now protected as national parks and reserved forests.

Assam has wildlife sanctuaries, the most prominent of which are two UNESCO World Heritage sites-the Kaziranga National Park, on the bank of the Brahmaputra River, and the Manas Wildlife Sanctuary, near the border with Bhutan. The Kaziranga is a refuge for the fast-disappearing Indian one-horned rhinoceros. The state is the last refuge for numerous other endangered and threatened species including the white-winged wood duck or *deohanh*, Bengal florican, black-breasted parrotbill, red-headed vulture, white-rumped vulture, greater adjutant, Jerdon's babbler, rufous-necked hornbill, Bengal tiger, Asian elephant, pygmy hog, gaur, wild water buffalo, Indian hog deer, hoolock gibbon, golden langur, capped langur, barasingha, Ganges river dolphin, Barca snakehead, Ganges shark, Burmese python, brahminy river turtle, black pond turtle, Asian forest tortoise, and Assam roofed turtle. Threatened species that are extinct in Assam include the gharial, a critically endangered fish-eating crocodilian, and the pink-headed duck(which may be extinct worldwide). For the state bird, the white-winged wood duck, Assam is a globally important area. In addition to the above, there are three other National Parks in Assam namely Dibru Saikhowa National Park, Nameri National Park and the Orang National Park.

Assam has conserved the one-horned Indian rhinoceros from near extinction, along with the pygmy hog, tiger and numerous species of birds, and it provides one of the last wild habitats for the Asian elephant. Kaziranga and Manas are both World Heritage Sites. The state contains Sal tree forests and forest products, much depleted from earlier times. A land of high rainfall, Assam displays greenery. The Brahmaputra River tributaries and oxbow lakes provide the region with hydrogeomorphic environment.

The state has the largest population of the wild water buffalo in the world. The state has the highest diversity of birds in India with around 820 species. With subspecies the number is as high as 946. The mammal diversity in the state is around 190 species.

Flora

Assam is remarkably rich in Orchid species and the Foxtail orchid is the state flower of Assam. The recently established Kaziranga National Orchid and Biodiversity Park boasts more than 500 of the estimated 1,314 orchid species found in India.

Geology

Assam has petroleum, natural gas, coal, limestone and other minor minerals such as magnetic quartzite, kaolin, sillimanites, clay and feldspar. A small quantity of iron ore is available in western districts. Discovered in 1889, all the major petroleum-gas reserves are in Upper parts. A recent USGS estimate shows 399 million barrels (63,400,000 m) of oil, 1,178 billion cubic feet (3.34×10 m) of gas and 67 million barrels (10,700,000 m) of natural gas liquids in the Assam Geologic Province.

The region is prone to natural disasters like annual floods and frequent mild earthquakes. Strong earthquakes were recorded in 1869, 1897, and 1950.

Languages

Languages of Assam (2011)

Assamese (48.38%)

Bengali (28.92%)

Hindi (6.73%)

Bodo (4.54%)

Sadri (2.29%)

Mishing (1.98%)

Nepali (1.91%)

Karbi (1.64%)

Kuki (0.11%)

Others (3.5%)

Assamese and Bodo are the major indigenous and official languages while Bengali is the official language in the three districts in the Barak Valley where Sylheti is the most spoken indigenous language. Bengali is the second most widely spoken language of the state, although a significant portion of those who are recorded speaking Bengali in the census do not actually speak Bengali, but instead speak closely related languages normally treated as dialects of Bengali, like Sylhetiand Rangpuri.

According to the language census of 2011 in Assam, out of a total population of around 31 million, Assamese is spoken by around half that number: 15 million. Although the number of speakers is growing, the percentage of Assam's population who have it as a mother tongue has fallen slightly.

The various Bengali dialects and closely related languages are spoken by around 9 million people in Assam, and the portion of the population that speaks these languages has grown slightly. Bodo is still the third most-spoken language

Traditionally, Assamese was the language of the common folk (of mixed origin – Austroasiatic, Tibeto-Burman, Prakrit) in the ancient Kamarupa kingdom and in the medieval kingdoms of Kamatapur, Kachari, Chutiya, Borahi, Ahom and Koch. Traces of the language are found in many poems by Luipa, Sarahapa, and others, in Charyapada (c. 7th–8th century AD). Modern dialects such as Kamrupi and Goalpariya are remnants of this language. Moreover, Assamese in its traditional form was used by the ethno-cultural groups in the region as lingua-franca, which spread during the stronger kingdoms and was required for economic integration. Localised forms of the language still exist in Nagaland and Arunachal Pradesh. The form used in upper Assam was enriched by the advent of Tai-Shans in the 13th century.

Linguistically modern Assamese traces its roots to the version developed by the American Missionaries based on the local form used near Sivasagar (Xiwôxagôr) district. Assamese (*Ôxômiya*) is a rich language due to its hybrid nature and unique characteristics of pronunciation and softness. Assamese literature is also one of the richest.

The word *Dimasa* etymologically translates to "Son of the big river " (Di- Water, ma- suffix for great, sa-sons), the river being the mighty Brahmaputra. The Dimasa word "Di" for water forms the root word for many of the major rivers of Assam and the North East India like Dikrang which means green river, Dikhow which means "fetched water", Diyung (huge river) etc. The Brahmaputra River is known as Dilao (long river) among the Dimasas. Many of the towns and cities in Assam and Nagaland derived their names from Dimasa words. For example, Dimapur (a capital of Dimasa Kingdom), Dispur, Hojai, Diphu and Khaspur.

Bodo is an ancient language of Assam. Spatial distribution patterns of the ethno-cultural groups, cultural traits and the phenomenon of naming all the major rivers in the North East Region with Bodo-Kachari words (e.g. Dihing, Dibru, Dihong, D/Tista, Dikrai, etc.) reveal that it was the most important language in the ancient times. Bodo is now spoken largely in the Western Assam (Bodo Territorial Council area). After years of neglect, now Bodo language is getting attention and its literature is developing. Other native languages of Tibeto-Burman origin and related to Bodo-Kachari are Deori, Mising, Karbi, Rabha, and Tiwa. Kukish is another native language of Assam belonging to the Tibeto-Burman group. However it does not belong to the Bodo-Kachari group.

There are approximately 564,000 Nepali speakers spread all over the state forming about 2.12% of Assam's total population according to 2001 census.

There are speakers of Tai languages in Assam. A total of six Tai language were spoken in Assam. Two are now extinct.

- Tai Phake
- Tai Aiton
- Khamti
- Khamyang (critically endangered)
- Ahom (extinct)
- Turung (extinct)

PEOPLE

People and Lifestyle: Assam is a mini-India if not more. The human landscape is as colourful as her physiography. This land has been the meeting ground of diverse ethnic groups and cultural streams since time immemorial. Throughout history, people of different stocks have been migrating into this land and merged into a common harmonious whole in a process of assimilation and fraternisation not to be seen much elsewhere in India.

The principal migrants have been the Austro-Asiatics, the Dravidians, the Tibeto-Burmans, the Mongoloids and the Aryans. The Austro-Asiatics, who were one of the earliest to arrive, initially lived in the Brahmaputra Valley, but were later pushed to the hills by the subsequent waves of migrants. The Khasis and Jaintias of present-day Meghalaya are said to be the descendants of this stock.

Next to come were the Dravidians, and the ethnological conjecture is that the Kaibarta and Bania communities of modern Assam are descendants of this group.

The Mongoloid migration to Assam took place at long intervals and from widely varied sources. They, in general, belong to the Tibeto-Burman family of the indo-Chinese group. The early waves of this group constituted the ancestors of the present-day Kacharis, Dimasas, Bodos, Rabhas and Lalungs, as also most of the tribes living in the hills neighbouring modern Assam.

The Kacharis are a powerful family and are today mostly known as the Bodos in the Brahmaputra Valley and Dimasas in the North Cachar Hills. The Koches on the other hand are said to be an admixture of the Dravidian and Mongoloid stocks. They are called Rajbangshis in the extreme western part of the State.

The Chutiyas in Upper Assam originally settled in the north-eastern tip of the region, but later gave way to make room for the Ahoms, who belonged to the Shan sub-section of the great indo-Chinese family.

The Mishings and the Karbis belong to the Tibeto-Burman stock, and inhabit the northern plains of Upper Assam and the Karbi hills respectively. The Khamits of extreme Upper Assam, as also the Naras, Phakiyals and Shyams (Man-Tai and Tai-Turung) belong to the Shan sub-section, and are believed to be groups who arrived much after the Ahoms.

Assam today has 16 Scheduled Castes and 23 Scheduled Tribes, with proposals for inclusion of more ethnic groups in the two categories still awaiting approval of the Centre.

The people of Assam inhabit a multi-ethnic, multi-linguistic and multi-religious society. They speak languages that belong to three main language groups: Austro-Asiatic, Tibeto-Burman and Indo-Aryan. The large number of ethnic and linguistic groups, the population composition and the peopling process in the state has led to it being called an "India in miniature".

Geographically Assam contains fertile river valleys surrounded by mountains. It is accessible from Tibet in the north (Bum La, Tse La, Tunga), across the Patkai (Diphu, Kumjawng, Hpungan, Chaukam, Pangsau, More-Tamu) and Myanmar across the Arakan Yoma (An, Taungup). In the west both the Brahmaputra valley and the Barak valley open widely to the Gangetic plains. It has been estimated that there were eleven major waves and streams of ethnolinguistic migrations over time.

Pre-historic

The earliest settlers were the Mon-Khmer speakers (Khasi, Synteng) (1) people from Southeast Asia. These people settled in the foothills but were pushed up into the hills (Khasi/Garo

Hills, Karbi Anglong, North Cachar Hills) by the second group of people that spoke Tibeto-Burmese (2) of the Eastern Himalayan, North Assam, Bodo and Naga groups of languages. These people are today identified as Monpas and Sherdukpens of Bhutan and Arunachal Pradesh; Mishings and Deuris of Upper Assam; the Bodo-Kachari groups scattered all over Assam and the Nagas of Karbi Anglong and North Cachar Hills.

Proto-historic and Ancient

The third major ingress into Assam are attributed to the Hindus (3) from North India into the Brahmaputra valley after 500 BC, and around the same time, from the Gangetic Delta of Bengal into the Barak valley. This signaled the dawn of the proto-Historic period and the immigration continued into the Ancient period, at the end of which the first Muslims (4), captive soldiers of the defeated Bakhtiar Khilji (in 1205), settled in the Hajo area.

Medieval

In the medieval times, the first Muslims (4), captive soldiers of the defeated Bakhtiar Khilji (in 1205), settled in the Hajo area. This was followed by the Ahoms (5) when Sukaphaa lead his group into Assam via the Pangsau pass in the Patkai from South China. The Ahoms were followed by the same ethnic people, but who were Buddhists (6), a stream that continued well into the colonial period. They are today the Khamti, Khamyang, Aiton, Phake and Turung peoples settled in Upper Assam.

Colonial and Post-independence

In the beginning of the colonial period in Assam after the First Anglo-Burmese War and the Treaty of Yandaboo (1826), the political instability led to the immigration of Kachin and Kuki-Chin people (7) into the region across the Patkai and Arakan Yoma. They constitute the Singphos in Upper Assam, and the Kuki-Chin tribes in Karbi Anglong and North Cachar Hills.

The beginning of tea plantations in Assam (1835) by the British led to settlements of Mundari speaking people (8) (Munda, Santal, Savara, Oraon, Gond etc. tribes). The beginning of British administration also led to a large influx of service holders and professionals from Bengal, Rajasthan, Nepal, etc. (9). To increase land productivity, the British encouraged Muslim peasants (10) from Mymensingh district of present-day Bangladesh to settle in Assam that began in 1901. The last major group to immigrate are the Bengali Hindu refugees (11) especially from the Sylhet district of Bangladesh following the Partition of India.

Inputs from these and other smaller groups have gone towards the building of a unique multi-ethnic socio-cultural situation. A temporal model of Peopling of Assam based on ethnolinguistic groups.

Social Formations

The process of social formation in Assam has been marked by simultaneous sanskritization and tribalization of different groups that settled in Assam, and best studied in three periods: (1) Pre-colonial, (2) Colonial and (3) Post-colonial periods.

Social History

Pre-historic Age: (a) Migration of Human races: The migration of different human races to the ancient land of Assam began two hundreds years before the birth of Christ. The Karbis, being the descendents of Austric race, are like the Columbus of Assam. The Khasis, Jayantias, Kukies, Lusais (Mizo) are all from this race.

The Kirats, being migrants from the western part of China, are from the Mongoloid race who speak Sino-Tibetan language. Bodo, Garo, Rabha, Deuries, Misings, Morans, Sutias, Dimasas and Koches (Rajbongshi), Lalung, Hajong are also from the same race. The assimilation started as both the races co-existed in the same geographical area. This is the background where the historic assimilation of Assamese nation-building process took place. Then the Kaibartas and Banias from Drabirian race migrated from the coast of Mediterranean came into assimilation more or less.

The name of this geographic area was Pragjyotishpur in the 4th - 5th centuries. King Mahiranga (Danaba) from the Mongoloid race was the first monarch of Pragjyotishpur. King Hatak(asur), Sambar(asur), Rambh(asur), Ghatak(asur) and King Narak(asur) reigned serially in the throne of Pragjyotishpur as the descendent of Mahiranga Danab. On the other hand the Aryans from Cocasian race migrated through the Gangetic Plain in the 1st century to the land of Pragjyotishpur.

The local king amongst the Mongolian majority society rehabilitated the Aryans, being the carrier of comparatively advanced religion and language-culture. In the presence of these people, the process of assimilation started long before the birth of Christ that has achieved a new acceleration. Narak(asur), the first monarch who was converted to Hindu religion, constructed the first temple and city at Kamakhya. As the king and the royal dynasty were converted to Hindu religion of the Aryans, the caste division also germinated in the tribal society of that time.

Middle Age The king and the Royal dynasty on one side formed a royal class with the Brahmin priest rehabilitated by them and on the other side the general people comprising the agri-slave, lower strata of the royal house formed the peasantry. After this stratification the first king of Barman dynasty reigned at Pragjyotishpur from 350 AD to 380 AD.

During this period, the name of Pragjyotishpur became Kamrup. Religious communalism penetrated to Kamrup in the last part of the reign of Salastambha dynasty (650 AD to 790 AD) and Pal dynasty (up to 1142 AD) after of the reign the Bhaskar Barman, the most powerful and the last king of Barman dynasty (he ruled till 650 AD).

Thus religious communalism took firm roots in Assam (the then Kamrup) which infiltrated along with the migration of Brahmin priests to Assam.

The Hindu religion was divided into different branches like Sakta, Saiba, Baishnaba during the time of the Indian king Chandra Gupta Maurya.

In 1228 AD, Tai speaker Sao Lung Sukapha of Mongolian race stepped on this land. During those period Kamrup was divided into four distinct zones such as Kam-peeth, Soumar-peeth, Ratna-peeth, and Swarna-peeth. Every zone was further divided into separate independent states under the rule of more than one tribal king. Sukapha established a powerful united feudal state through his broad strategy of "establishing one state by unifying seven states" within Kamrup. Since then, Kamrup became to be known as Asom. The presence of the Tais has done the irregular process of social assimilation more forceful in between the migrant races such as Austrics, Mongoloids, Drabirs and Caucasians.

The relation and the synthesis among the different tribes, as being isolated before, were developed with the pace of the development of agriculture and communication system under the patronage of modern administration and military structure of Tai-Ahoms. Thus Assamese became the link language amongst the peoples who speak different dialects.

At the same time, a handful of rich class of businessmen and merchants developed. This brought about the development of society to a certain stage during the six hundred years of Ahom rule.

On the other hand, at the Kam-peeth and Ratna-peeth a series of invasion took place under the commands of Muhammad Ghauri, Muhammad Bin-Bakhtier, Giasuddin, Nasirudin and Tughril Khan prior to the arrival of the Tais. Kamrup was still capable of keeping its sovereignty invincible. The Muslim captives of the war who were compelled to stay here after the wars have been assimilated into Assamese society. Under the leadership of Ahom administration, the sovereignty of Assam was preserved resisting the invasion of Asia-victor the Mughals for seventeen times with the help of different tribes of Assam.

During the time of Ahom administration, the Sikh religious priest Tegbahadur and the Muslim religious scholar Azan Fakir came to Assam and Srimanta Sankardeva, the preceptor of puritan Hinduism, was born in Assam. As the religious preceptors started the act of publicity of their religions, the language of royal house spread amongst the subjects. Again, the practice of upkeeping the history (Buranji) and the patronage from the royal house have made the language and literature richer.

During this period the religious communalism became strong enough inside classified society which was planted long before. However, till the time of His Highness Pratap Chadra Singh, the tribal system of royal administration was prevalent. But the tribal traditions became eroded due to the imposition of land surveying, population census, the introduction of PAIK system which crushed the tribal demography, the commencement of more developed feudal system and lastly the import and rehabilitation of Hindu religious Brahman-priest from India.

The contradiction between the ruling class consisting of the King, the royal family, the royal officers from the ministers to the Chamuas and the general peasantry comprising of Paike, Slave, House-man and war prisoners became intensified. Thereafter, the conflicts of the general feudal peasantry with the ruling class reflected through the Moamaria rebellion (1769-1826) in the form of religious communalism became intensified. The Ahom administrative system was crushed due to the conflict between the ruler and the subjects.

Again, the assimilated social life was isolated. The massive loss of life occurred and these undecided peoples' uprising caused the famine that made the total social life of Assam very weak. On the one hand the Burmese arrived accepting the call of Sarbananda Singha and on the other hand the British came in response to the invitation of Gaurinath Singha. There were enormous loss of life and property due to the invasion of these two foreign powers one after another. The Burmese occupied Assam for four years from 1822 to1826 AD after she was invaded thrice in 1817,1819 and 1821. The Assamese society was in such an era of decay that all efforts, individual and collective, for the resistance against the Burmese could not produce any positive result.

The Assam Rifles are an Indian paramilitary force. Currently there are 33 battalions of Assam Rifles under the control of the Indian Ministry of Home Affairs (MHA).

The first form of what is now the Assam Rifles was Cachar Levy, a paramilitary police force of 750 men that was formed under British colonial rule in 1835. It was formed as police unit to protect settlements against tribal raids and other assaults as British rule slowly moved towards the north. In 1870 the existing elements were merged into three Assam Military Police battalions in the Lushai Hills (later 1st battalion), Lakhimpur (2nd battalion) and Naga Hills (3rd battalion). A fourth battalion was formed 1915 in Imphal.

During the World War I, Assam Military Police troopers were part of the Indian forces that fought for Britain in Europe and Middle East. The name Assam Rifles was assigned in 1917 as recognition of their part in the war. After the war they served in Northern India against rebellions and riots.

During the World War II, the Assam Rifles helped manage the influx of refugees coming from Burma fleeing the Japanese advance in 1942. They also organized a resistance group called Victor Force or V-Force on the Burmese border to harass Japanese communications. Troopers also served in the battle of Kohima and earned numerous unit citations.

Between the end of World War II and Indian independence, the Assam Rifles were composed of 5 battalions that were one part of the civil police under the Assam Inspector General of Police. After independence, the Indian government assigned the Assam Rifles its own Director General.

As the numbers of the force and the number of battalions gradually increased, the rank of the force commander was also upgraded until now it is that of lieutenant general.

One of the tasks of the unit was to keep order in the aftermath of the 1950 Assam earthquake and assist in resettlement. In October 1962 the Assam Rifles were the frontline troops in the beginning of the Chinese-Indian War. The Assam Rifles also maintained their peacekeeping roles in the Northern India in the face of tribal unrest and insurgency.

The Assam Rifles also handle medical assistance, aid in basic education, assist in reconstruction and agriculture and handles communications in remote areas.

BODO PEOPLE

The Bodos pronounced BO-ROs are an ethnic and linguistic community, early settlers of Assam in the North-East India. According to the 1991 census, there are 1.2 million Bodos in Assam which makes for 5.3% of the total population in the state. Bodos belong to a larger group of ethnicity called the Bodo-Kachari. The Bodos are recognized as a plains tribe in the Sixth Schedule of the Indian Constitution. Kokrajhar town is considered the nerve centre of the Bodos.

The Bodo-Kachari: The Bodos represents one of the largest of the 18 ethnic sub-groups within the Bodo-Kacharis group, first classified in the 19th century. Bodos have settled in most areas of North-East India, and parts of Nepal. Among the 18 groups mentioned by Endle, the Mech in Western Assam, the Bodo in central Assam, the Dimasa and Hojai to the north of Cachar Hills, and the Sonowal and Thengal in the eastern part of the Brahmaputra river are closely related. The others have been either Hinduized (*e.g.*, Koch, Sarania), or have developed separate identities (*e.g.*, Garo).

The Bodo People: The Bodos represents one of the largest ethnic and linguistic groups of the Brahmaputra valley. Typical Bodo last names (surname) are Bargayary, Basumatary, Bodosa, Boro, Brahma, Bwiswmuthiary, Dwimary, Goyary, Ishlary, Ishwary, Khaklary, Mushahary, Narzary, Owary, Sargwary, Sibigry and Wary. The 1971 census report indicated Bodos being the 8th largest scheduled-tribe (ST) group in India. Close to 1 million people speak Bodo language.

The Bodo language is derived from Tibeto-Burmese family of languages. Although, Roman script and Assamese script were used in the past. Recently, Bodos adopted the Devanagari script. According to some scholars, the Bodo language had a script of its own called Deodhai.

Very early on, Bodos may have introduced rice cultivation, tea plantation, pig and poultry farming, and silkworm rearing in the North East India. The traditional favourite drink of the Bodos is Zu Mai (Zu:wine, Mai:rice). Rice is a staple of the Bodos and is often accompanied by a non vegetarian dish such as fish or pork. Traditionally Bodos are non-vegetarians.

Weaving is another integral part of Bodo culture. Many families rear their own silkworms, the cocoons of which are then spun into silk. Bodo girls learn to weave from a young age, and no Bodo courtyard is complete without a loom. Most women weave their own Dokhnas (the traditional dress of the Bodo women) and shawls. The Bodos are also expert craftsmen in bamboo products.

Religion: In the past, Bodos worshipped their forefathers. In recent years, Bodos practice Bathouism, Christianity or Hinduism or Islam. Bathouism is a form worshipping forefathers called Obonglaoree. The siju plant (belonging to the Euphorbia genus), is taken as the symbol of Bathou and worshiped. In the Bodo Language "Ba" means five and "thou" means deep. Five is a significant number in the Bathou religion.

A clean surface near home or courtyard could be an ideal for worship.

Usually, one pair of Betelnut called 'goi' and betel leaf called 'pathwi' could be used as offering. On some occasion, worship offering could include rice, milk, and sugar. For the Kherai Puja, the most important festival of the Bodos, the altar is placed in the rice field. Other important festivals of the Bodos include Garja, Hapsa Hatarnai, Awnkham Gwrlwi Janai, Bwisagu and Domashi.

Despite the advance of Hinduism amongst the Bodos, mainstream Indian practices such as caste and dowry are not practiced by the majority of Bodo Hindus who follow a set of rules called Brahma Dharma.

The Bodos Now: The Bodos struggled for self-determination in late 80's under the leadership of Upendra Nath Brahma, who is now regarded as the father of the Bodos (Bodo-Fa). After a protracted struggle to save tribal belts and block, Bodo culture, language and identity, the Bodos have been granted the Bodoland Territorial Council, an autonomous administrative body that will have within its jurisdiction the present district of Kokrajhar and adjoining areas.

The movement for autonomy was headed by the All Bodo Students Union (ABSU) and an armed militant group called Bodo Liberation Tigers (BLT). Following the establishment of the BTC, the BLT have come overground.

In 2006 Assam Assembly elections, the former BLT members under Hagrama Mohilary formed an alliance with the Indian National Congress and came to power in Dispur. Educational and job opportunity remain biggest problem for Bodos. In Assam, illegal immigrant still occupy tribal belts and blocks. In a nutshell, many players came and gone, game changed, however, Bodoland never materialized.

Bodoland

Bodoland is an area located in the north bank of Brahmaputra river in the state of Assam in north east region of India, by the foothills of Bhutan and Arunachal Pradesh; inhabited predominantly by Bodo language speaking ethnic group. Currently the map of Bodoland includes the Bodoland Territorial Areas District (BTAD) administered by an autonomous Bodoland Territorial Council (BTC). The map of Bodoland overlaps with the districts of Kokrajhar, Baksa, Chirang and Udalguri in state of Assam. At present, Kokrajhar town serves as the headquarter (capital) of Bodoland.

Bodoland Movement: The early history of Bodos is largely unknown. By definition, Bodos (pronounced BO-ROs) do not display tribalistic culture or rituals in that they do not live in caves or jungles or go hunting wild animals. For centuries majority Bodos remained as farmers, cultivators, and peace loving society. Like many cultures in the world today, Bodos are also ethnocentric or nationalist society. Cultural assimilation with Assamese was not productive.

In brief, before the British Raj, Bodo-kachari Kingdom may have included a vast area extending far and beyond Assam, a small province in the North-East India. History suggest that Dimapur was the capital of Bodo-Kachari kingdom. The British-India colonial rulers effectively adapted divide and rule policy for over 300 years.

It is likely that Bodo-Kachari were lagging behind their fellow Indians in terms of education and employability. Since the time of British Raj, Assam is known to produce oil and natural gas, and Assam tea. Before independence (1947), North-East India was a remote place, a land that was inaccessible due to heavy rain and forestation. Compared to other parts of India, such as West Bengal and Maharastra, Education came to North East India late, as late as after the independence.

Even after India obtained independence, most official jobs were performed by immigrants from West Bengal, East Bengal (now Bangladesh), and other parts of British-India. When India obtained independence, Bodos were not represented by any group. In the process, like the Khasis (Hills-tribe), Bodos were given opportunity to take advantage of scheduled-tribe (ST, plains). This process lead to the creation of tribal belts and blocks, protected lands meant for farming and grazing, specifically for Bodo people.

Plains Tribals Council

In the early 60's the Plains Tribals Council of Assam (PTCA), a political party representing Bodos (pronounced BO-ROs) and other plains tribals of Assam realized that tribal belts and blocks were gradually being acquired by rich landlords or new immigrants through illegal means. Moreover, Bodos had little or no access to economic aid that were given by the central government. Without economic package to the Bodo dominated areas, education was a distant cry. In those days, there were hardly any roads that connected Bodo dominated area to the main cities of Assam.

These were several reasons for which, in 1967, PTCA demanded a Union Territory called Udayachal, to be carved out of Assam. The proposed Udayachal map included mainly those areas that was known as tribal belts and blocks. The creation of tribal belts and blocks (for scheduled-tribes) was a mechanism to protect farming and grazing lands mainly from rich landlord and illegal immigrants.

The demand for Udayachal never materialized. Many government came and gone, players changed and so did the game. By the end of 70's it became clear that Bodos had a little or no influence in the Indian political process. Specifically, in Assam Bodos areas were neglected. Neglects included diverting and misuse of tribal-plan funds. For similar reasons, Khasis and Garos, carved out Meghalaya from Assam. In the late 80's, All Bodo Students' Union's (ABSU) became very concerned about decades of neglects. ABSU and Bodo political parties jointly moved and demanded a separate state, called Bodoland.

All Bodo Students' Union (ABSU)

The official Bodoland Movement for an independent state of Bodoland started on March 2, 1987 under the leadership of Upendranath Brahma of ABSU. The ABSU created a political organization, the Bodo Peoples' Action Committee (BPAC), to spearhead the movement. The ABSU/BPAC movement began with the slogan "Divide Assam 50-50". The ABSU/BPAC leadership of the movement ended with the bipartite Bodo Accord of February 20, 1993 and the creation of the BAC. The accord soon collapsed amidst a vertical split in ABSU and other Bodo political parties brought about mainly by the split between S.K. Bwiswmuthiary and Premsingh Brahma, and violence erupted in Bodo areas leading to a displacement of over 70,000 people.

Illegal immigration remains a chronic problem for Assam. Notably, before the ABSU movement for Bodoland, the All Assam Students Union (AASU) launched agitation to stop illegal immigration. This long agitation by AASU provided initial impetus for Bodoland movement. One of the main objectives of the ABSU movement was to save tribal belts and blocks, and Bodo dominated areas from the illegal immigrants. Second, to establish educational institutions and create job opportunities, improve quality of daily life, and bring parity with Assamese folks. However, these objectives never materialized.

Bodo Students Plights

Even after independence, for several decades, higher education was out of reach for most Bodos. Universities and higher educational institutes are located in far away places such as Gauhati (now called Guwahati), Shillong, or Dibrugarh. Moreover, year after year majority Bodo students were denied admissions in Cotton College, Assam Agricultural University, Assam Engineering College and Gauhati University.

In addition, even after obtaining a college degree, Bodos had limited or no job opportunities. These reasons fueled disappointment and anger among Bodo students. Although, Bodos were given ST quota, most of those jobs or opportunities went unfilled. Every office in Assam were filled with Assamese speaking folks, from officers down to peons. Creating a better educational opportunities for Bodos became first goal for ABSU's. However, as All Assam Students Union's (AASU) agitation to drive out illegal immigrants (year 1979-85) was slowing down, the demand for a separate state, called Bodoland was gaining momentum.

Bodo Liberation Tigers Force

The creation of Gorkhaland, Jharkhand and Uttarranchal serve as good examples of Indian democracy and political maturity. In contrast, the Bodo Accord has not brought noticeable changes to Bodoland in terms of education, job opportunity, business development, or improvement of existing institutions, roads, and communications. For these reasons, BTLF continued to agitate for a separate state within Assam. Nevertheless, this phase of the movement ended with the Memorandum of Settlement with the BLTF on February 10, 2003, and the establishment of the Bodoland Territorial Council

(BTC) under the Sixth Sechedule of the Constitution of India.

The BLTF laid down their weapons on December 6, 2003 and its chief, Hagrama Mohilary, was sworn in as the Chief Executive Member (CEM) of the interim BTC on December 7, 2003. The BLTF joined hands with the ABSU to form a political party, the BPPF, but soon parted ways in 2005 at the time of the BTC elections. After the elections Mohilary consolidated his powers. The success of his faction in the 2006 Assam Assembly Elections has created a situation in which the Bodos under the leadership of Hagrama Mohilary has considerable influence in the Government of Assam for the first time in history.

Bodoland Autonomous Council (BAC)

The Bodoland Autonomous Council (BAC) was formed after the Bodo Accord.

Bodoland Territorial Council (BTC)

The Bodoland Territorial Council (BTC) is a 46-member body established according to the Memorandum of Settlement (MoS) of February 10, 2003. The first elections for the BTC were held on May 13, 2005. Of the 46 members, 40 are elected, and the rest nominated. The BTC could have not more than 12 executive members each of whom looks after a specific area of control called somisthi. The area under the BTC jurisdiction is called the Bodo Territorial Autonomous District (BTAD). The Council enjoys autonomy and control over departments specified in the MoS, but it does not control the district administration.

The BTAD consists of four contiguous districts-Kokrajhar, Baska, Udalguri and Chirang-carved out of eight existing districts-Dhubri, Kokrajhar, Bongaigaon, Barpeta, Nalbari, Kamrup, Darrang and Sonitpur-an area of 27,100 km^2 (35% of Assam).

Despite the Bodo accord, neglects remain, no economic parity is apparent. Whether the BTC addressed the issues of Bodo self-determination is still an open question. This was the first instance that guarantees for the hill tribes under the Sixth Schedule of the Constitution of India has been extended to the plains tribes.

Bodo Sahitya Sabha

On November 16, 1952, the Bodo Sahitya Sabha, the vanguard of Bodo language and literature, was founded at Basugaon, in the district of Kokrajhar, Assam consisting of representatives of Assam, West Bengal, Meghalaya, Nagaland, Tripura and Nepal in abroad.

Early Work: After India obtained independence, a critical mass of Bodo intellectuals realized the need for preservation of Bodo language. Many early Bodo authors studied in schools and colleges, where medium of instruction was either Assamese or Bangla. Bodo intellectuals felt that Bodo language must be preserved and developed at par with Assamese and Bangla languages. Bodo people realized very late that the education was the key component to the overall development of Bodo people and their language. After prolonged struggle and determination of the Bodo Sahitya Sabha (Bodo Literary Organization), the Bodo language was introduced as a medium of instruction at primary level in 1963 and then at secondary level in 1968. Bodo language and literature has been recognized as one of the Major Indian Languages (MIL) in Gauhati, Dibrugarh and North-Eastern Hill Universities. In 1985, Bodo has been recognized as an associated state official language of Assam.

Recent Development: Now the language has attained a position of pride with the opening of the Post-Graduate Courses in Bodo language and literature in the University of Gauhati in 1996. Moreover, under the aegis of the commission for Scientific and Technical terminology, HRD Ministry, the Govt. of India, the Bodo Sahitya Sabha is preparing more than forty thousand scientific and technical terms in Bodo language. Further, it is promised, the Sahitya Academy would accord "Bhasa Sonman" (respect for language) to the Bodo language and literature as an initial token of full-fledged recognition to it. Furthermore, the Govt. of India, in principle, has recognized the necessity of inclusion of the Bodo language and literature in the Eighth Schedule of the Constitution of India.

Contributions: Moreover the Bodo Sahitya Sabha has to its credit a large number of books on prose, poetry, drama, short story, novel, biography, travelogue, children's literature & criticism.

2

Culture and Society

CULTURE

Assamese culture is traditionally a hybrid one developed due to assimilation of ethno-cultural groups of Austric, Tibeto-Burman and Tai origin in the past. Therefore, both local elements or the local elements in Sanskritised forms are distinctly found. The major milestones in evolution of Assamese culture are:

Dakhinpat Satra of Majuli

- Assimilation in the Kamarupa Kingdom for almost 700 years (under the Varmans for 300 years, Salastambhas and Palas for each 200 years).
- Establishment of the Chutiya dynasty in the 12th century in eastern Assam and assimilation for next 400 years.

- Establishment of the Ahom dynasty in the 13th century AD and assimilation for next 600 years.
- Assimilation in the Koch Kingdom (15th–16th century AD) of western Assam and Kachari Kingdom (12th–18th century AD) of central and southern Assam.

Presenting **Gayan Bayan** *in Majuli, the Neo-Vaishnavite Cultural heritage of Assam*

- Vaishnava Movement led by Srimanta Shankardeva (*Sonkordeu*) and its contribution and cultural changes. Vaishanava Movement, the 15th century religio-cultural movement under the leadership of great Srimanta Sankardeva (Sonkordeu) and his disciples have provided another dimension to Assamese culture. A renewed Hinduisation in local forms took place, which was initially greatly supported by the Koch and later by the Ahom Kingdoms. The resultant social institutions such as *namghar* and *sattra* (the Vaishnav Monasteries) have become part of Assamese way life. The movement contributed greatly towards language, literature and performing and fine arts.

The modern culture was influenced by events in the British and the Post-British Era. The language was standardised by the American BaptistMissionaries such as Nathan Brown, Dr. Miles Bronson and local pundits such as Hemchandra Barua with the form available in the Sibsagar(*Sivasagar*) District (the ex-nerve centre of the Ahom Kingdom).

Increasing efforts of standardisation in the 20th century alienated the localised forms present in different areas and with the less-assimilated ethno-cultural groups (many source-cultures).

However, Assamese culture in its hybrid form and nature is one of the richest, still developing and in true sense is a 'cultural system' with sub-systems. Many source-cultures of Assamese cultural-system are still surviving either as sub-systems or as sister entities, e.g. the ; Bodo or Karbi or Mishing. It is important to keep the broader system closer to its roots and at the same time to focus on development of the sub-systems.

Some of the common and unique cultural traits in the region are peoples' respect towards areca-nut and betel leaves, symbolic (gamosa, arnai, etc.), traditional silk garments (e.g. mekhela chador, traditional dress of Assamese women) and towards forefathers and elderly. Moreover, great hospitality and bamboo culture are common.

CULTURE OF ASSAM

The culture of Assam is traditionally a hybrid one, developed due to cultural assimilation of different ethno-cultural groups under various political-economic systems in different periods of history.

Historical perspective

The roots of Assamese culture go back almost two thousand years when the first cultural assimilation took place between Austro-asiaticand Tibeto-Burman groups. There were three waves of cultural assimilation in Assam. First, it was the Tibeto-Burman ethnic groups which had arrived from Tibet, Yunnan and Sinchuan provinces of China who mixed with the scarcely present aboriginal Austric people like the Khasi and Jaintia. Then there was a wave of Indo-Aryans from Northern India, which brought the Vedic culture and Hinduism into Assam. The last wave of migration was that of the Ahoms(Tai/Shan) who added another chapter to the Assamese culture. The Ahoms later on brought some more Indo-Aryans like the Assamese

Brahmins and Ganaks and Assamese Kayasthas to Assam.

According to the epic *Mahabharata* and on the basis of local folk lore, people of Assam (Kiratas) probably lived in a strong kingdom under the Himalayas in the era before Jesus Christ, which led to an early assimilation of various Tibeto-Burman and Autro-asiatic ethnic groups on a greater scale. Typical naming of the rivers and spatial distribution of related ethno-cultural groups also support this theory. Thereafter, western migrations of Indo-Aryans such as those of various branches of Irano-Scythians and Nordics along with mixed northern Indians (the ancient cultural mix already present in northern Indian states such as Magadha enriched the aboriginal culture and under certain stronger politico-economic systems, Sanskritisation and Hinduisation intensified and became prominent. Such an assimilated culture therefore carries many elements of source cultures, of which exact roots are difficult to trace and are a matter for research. However, in each of the elements of Assamese culture, i.e. language, traditional crafts, performing arts, festivities and beliefs, either indigenous local elements or the indigenous local elements in a Sanskritised forms are always present.

It is believed that Assamese culture developed its roots over 750 years as the country of Kamarupa during the first millennium AD. The first 300 years of Kamarupa was under the great Varman dynasty, 250 years under the Mlechchha dynasty and 200 years under the Pala dynasty. The records of many aspects of the language, traditional crafts (silk, lac, gold, bronze, etc.) are available in different forms. When the Tai-Shans entered the region in 1228 under the leadership of Sukaphaa to establish Ahom kingdom in Assam for the next 600 years, again a new chapter of cultural assimilation was written, and thus the modern form of Assamese culture developed. The original Tai-Shans assimilated with the local culture, adopted the language on one hand and on the other also influenced the culture with the elements from their own. Similarly the Chutiya kingdom in eastern Assam, the Koch Kingdom in western Assam and the medieval Kachari and

Jaintia kingdomsin southern Assam provided stages for assimilation at different intensities and with different cultural-mixes.

The Vaishanav Movement, a 15th-century religio-cultural movement under the leadership of Srimanta Sankardeva and his disciples, have provided another dimension to Assamese culture. A renewed Hinduisation in local forms took place, which was initially greatly supported by the Koch and later by the Ahom Kingdoms. The resultant social institutions such as *namghar* and *sattra - the Vaishnav Hermitage* have become part of the Assamese way of life. The movement contributed greatly towards language, literature and performing and fine arts. On many occasions, the Vaishnav Movement attempted to introduce alien cultural attributes and modify the way of life of the common people. *Brajavali*, a language specially created by introducing words from other Indian languages, failed as a language but left its traces on the Assamese language. Moreover, new alien rules were also introduced changing people's food habits and other aspects of cultural life. This had a greater impact on the alienation of many local ethno-cultural and political groups in the later periods.

During periods when strong politico-economic systems that emerged under powerful dynasties, greater cultural assimilation created common attributes of Assamese culture, while under less powerful politico-economic systems or during political disintegration, more localised attributes were created with spatial differentiation. Time-factors for such integrations and differentiations have also played an important role along with the position of individual events in the entire series of events.

With a strong base of tradition and history, modern Assamese culture is greatly influenced by various events those took place in under British rule of Assam and in the Post-British Era. The language was standardised by American Missionaries according to that of the Sibsagar District, the nerve centre of the Ahom politico-economic system while a renewed Sanskritisation was increasingly adopted for developing Assamese language and grammar . A new wave of Western and northern Indian influence was apparent in the performing arts and literature.

Due to increasing efforts of standardisation in the 19th and 20th century, the localised forms present in different districts and also among the remaining source-cultures with the less-assimilated ethno-cultural groups have seen greater alienation. However, Assamese culture in its hybrid form and nature is one of the richest and is still under development.

Composition and characteristics

Assamese culture in its true sense today is a 'cultural system' composed of different sub-systems. It is more interesting to note that even many of the source-cultures of Assamese culture are still surviving either as sub-systems or as sister entities. In broader sense, therefore, the Assamese cultural system incorporates its source-cultures and However, it is also important to keep the broader system closer to its roots.

Elements

Symbolism

Symbolism is an important part of Assamese culture. Various elements are being used to represent beliefs, feelings, pride, identity, etc. Symbolism is an ancient cultural practice in Assam, which is still very important for the people. *Tamulpan*, *Xorai* and *Gamosa* are three important symbolic elements in Assamese culture.

Tamul-paan (the areca nut and betel leaves) or *guapan* (gua from *kwa*) are considered as the offers of devotion, respect and friendship. It is an ancient tradition and is being followed since time-immemorial with roots in the aboriginal Austric culture.

Xorai, a traditional symbol of Assam, is a manufactured bell-metal object and an article of great respect and is used as a container-medium while performing respectful offerings. It is an offering tray with a stand at the bottom similar to those found in East and South East Asia. There are xorais with or without a cover on the top. Traditionally xorai are made of bell metal although nowadays they can be made from brass and/or silver. Hajo and Sarthebari are the most important centres of traditional bell-metal and brass crafts including xorais. Xorais are used:

as an offering tray for tamul-pan (betel nuts and betel leaves) to guests as a sign of welcome and thanks.

as an offering tray for food and other items placed in front of the altar(naamghar)for blessing by the Lord.

as a decorative symbol in traditional functions such as during Bihu dances.

as a gift to a person of honour during felicitations.

The Gamosa is an article of great significance for the people of Assam. Literally translated, it means 'something to wipe the body with' (*Ga*=body, *mosa*=to wipe); interpreting the word "gamosa" as the body-wiping towel is misleading. It is generally a white rectangular piece of cloth with primarily a red border on three sides and red woven motifs on the fourth (in addition to red, other colors are also used). Though it is used daily to wipe the body after a bath (an act of purification), the use is not restricted to this. It is used by the farmer as a waistcloth (*tongali*) or a loincloth (*suriya*); a Bihu dancer wraps it around the head with a fluffy knot. It is hung around the neck at the prayer hall and was thrown over the shoulder in the past to signify social status. Guests are welcomed with the offering of a *gamosa* and *tamul* (betel nut) and elders are offered *gamosas* (*bihuwaan*) during Bihu. It is used to cover the altar at the prayer hall or cover the scriptures. An object of reverence is never placed on the bare ground, but always on a *gamosa*. One can therefore, very well say, that the *gamosa* symbolizes the life and culture of Assam.

Significantly the *gamosa* is used equally by all irrespective of religious and ethnic backgrounds.

At par with Gamosa, there are beautifully woven symbolic

clothes with attractive graphic designs being used by different cultural sub-systems and ethno-cultural groups as well.

There were various other traditional symbolic elements and designs in use, which are now found only in literature, art, sculpture, architecture, etc. or used for only religious purposes (in particular occasions). The typical designs of *assamese-lion, dragon, flying-lion*, etc. were used for symbolising various purposes and occasions.

Festivals

There are several important indigenous traditional festivals in Assam. Bihu is the most celebrated festival among all. Indigenous traditional festivals are celebrated every year around different corners of Assam.

A group of Bihu dancers.

Bihu is a series of three prominent festivals of Assam. Primarily a festival celebrated to mark the seasons and the significant points of a cultivator's life over a yearly cycle, in recent times the form and nature of celebration has changed with the growth of urban centers. Three Bihus are celebrated: *rongali*, celebrated with the coming of spring and the beginning of the sowing season; *kongali*, the barren bihu when the fields are lush but the barns are empty; and the *bhogali*, the thanksgiving when the crops have been harvested and the barns are full. Rongali, kongali & bhogali bihu are also known as 'bohag bihu', 'kati bihu' & 'magh bihu' respectively. The day before the each bihu is known as 'uruka'. There are unique features of each bihu. The first day of 'rongali bihu' is called 'Goru bihu' (the bihu of the cows). On this day the cows are taken to the nearby rivers or ponds to be bathed with special care. Traditionally, cows are respected as sacred animals by the people of Assam. Bihu songs and Bihu dance are associated to *rongali* bihu.

Youth wearing Assamese traditional costumes

Bwisagu is a very popular seasonal festival of the Bodo of Assam. Bwisagu means start of the new year. Baisagu is a Boro word which originated from the word "Baisa" which means year or age, and "Agu" that means starting or start

Ali-Ai-Ligang is the spring festival of the Mising people of Assam, India. The name of the festival is made up of three terms, 'Ali', root and seed, 'Ai', fruit and 'Ligang', to sow. Bohuwa dance is festival of Sonowal Kacharis of Assam, India.

Music

Assam, being the home to many ethnic groups and different cultures, is rich in folk music. The indigenous folk music has in turn influenced the growth of a modern idiom, that finds expression in the music of such artists are Jyoti Prasad Agarwala, Bishnuprasad Rabha, Parvati Prasad Baruva, Bhupen Hazarika, Nirmalendu Choudhury & Utpalendu Choudhury, Pratima Barua Pandey, Luit Konwar Rudra Baruah, Parvati Prasad Baruva, Jayanta Hazarika, Khagen Mahanta, Beauty Sarma Baruah.

Among the new generation Zubeen Garg, Angaraag Mahanta, Kalpana Patowary, Joi Barua, Jitul Sonowal and Manoj Borah are well known.

And other than traditional assamese music assam's capital city Guwahati have become country's capital for rock music other than Shillong. A number of talented rock bands have formed showcasing their talents around the world.

Traditional crafts

Assam has maintained a rich tradition of various traditional crafts for more than two thousand years. Presently, Cane and bamboo craft, bell metal and brass craft, silk and cotton weaving, toy and mask making, pottery and terracotta work, wood craft, jewellery making, musical instruments making, etc. are remained as major traditions. Historically, Assam also excelled in making boats, traditional guns and gunpowder, colours and paints, articles of lac, traditional building materials, utilities from iron, etc.

Cane and bamboo craft provide the most commonly used utilities in daily life, ranging from household utilities, weaving accessories, fishing accessories, furniture, musical instruments to building construction materials. Traditional utilities and symbolic articles made from bell metal and brass are found in every Assamese household.

The Xorai and bota have been in use for centuries to offer gifts to respected persons and are two prominent symbolic elements. Hajo and Sarthebari are the most important centres of traditional bell-metal and brass crafts. Assam is the home of several types of silks, the most prominent and prestigious being Muga, the natural golden silk is exclusive only to Assam. Apart from Muga, there are other two varieties called Pat, a creamy-bright-silver coloured silk and Eri, a variety used for manufacturing warm clothes for winter. Apart from Sualkuchi, the centre for the traditional silk industry, in almost every parts of the Brahmaputra Valley, rural households produce silk and silk garments with excellent embroidery designs. Moreover, various ethno-cultural groups in Assam make different types of cotton garments with unique embroidery designs and wonderful colour combinations.

Moreover, Assam possesses unique crafts of toy and mask making mostly concentrated in the Vaishnav Hermitage, pottery and terracotta work in Western Assam districts and wood craft, iron craft, jewellery, etc. in many places across the region. However we can see assam populated because of these.

Traditional clothes and fabric of the Assamese include Suriya, Pirawn, Gamusa, Jaapi, Mekhela Sadawr, Riha, Tongali.

ASSAMESE CINEMA

Assamese cinema also known as Jollywood cinemas, is cinema in the Assamese language, watched primarily in Assam, India. The industry was born in 1935 when Jyoti Prasad Agarwala released his movie *Joymoti*. Since then Assamese cinema has developed a slow-paced, sensitive style, especially with the movies of Bhabendra Nath Saikia and Jahnu Barua. The industry is sometimes called Jollywood, named for Agarwala and his Jyoti Chitraban Film Studio.

Despite its long history and its artistic successes, for a state that has always taken its cinema seriously, Assamese cinema has never really managed to break through on the national scene despite its film industry making a mark in the National Awards over the years. Although the beginning of the 21st century has seen Bollywood-style Assamese movies hitting the screen, the industry has not been able to compete in the market, significantly overshadowed by the larger industries such as Bollywood.

History

1930s

The origins of Assamese cinema can be traced back to Rupkonwar Jyotiprasad Agarwala, who was also a noted poet, playwright, composer and freedom fighter. He was instrumental in the production of the first Assamese Film *Joymati* in 1935, under the banner of Chitralekha Movietone.

Due to the lack of trained technicians, Jyotiprasad, while making his maiden film, shouldered the added responsibilities as the script writer, producer, director, choreographer, editor, set and costume designer, lyricist and music director. The film, completed with a budget of 60,000 rupees was released on 10 March 1935.

The picture failed. Like so many early Indian films, the negatives and complete prints of *Joymati* are missing. Some effort has been made privately by Altaf Mazid to restore and subtitle whatever is left of the prints. Despite the significant financial loss from *Joymati*, the second picture *Indramalati* was filmed between 1937 and 1938 finally released in 1939. Pramathesh Barua released his Assamese version of *Devdas (1937 film)* in 1937. It was the last of the 3 language version following Bengali and Hindi.

1940s

Agarwala made another film after a lapse of two years titled *Indramalati*. It was his second and last film. The eminent composer and singer of Assam Bhupen Hazarika, played a prominent role in the play. With the passing away of Jyotiprasad, the Assamese film scene witnessed a temporary lull for about a couple of years. But things changed with the onset of World War II, Taking advantage of this, Rohini Kr. Baruah made a film on a relevant historical topic called *Manomati* in 1941. It was followed by films like Parvati Prasad Baruwa's *Rupahi* (1946), Kamal Narayan Choudhury's *Badan Barphukan* (1947), Phani Sharma's *Siraj*, Asit Sen's *Biplabi*, Prabin Phukan's *Parghat* and Suresh Goswami's *Runumi*.

1950s

In the 1950s, *Piyali Phukan* went on to win a National award.The movie was produced by Gama Prasad Agarwalla under the aegis of Rup Jyoti Productions. The film was directed by Phani Sharma and music was composed by Bhupen Hazarika. The film was about the life of the freedom fighter Piyali Phukan, who stood against the British Rule. He was executed by the British on charges of treason. This film technically was advanced for that time. In 1955, a new talent Nip Barua made his directorial debut with *Smrit Paras*. His subsequent films *Mak Aaru Moram* and *Ranga Police* won many state awards and the silver medal at the national level. Bhupen Hazarika also produced and directed his first film *Era Bator Sur*. Prabhat Mukherjee made a film on the universality of motherhood, *Puberun* (1959), which was shown in the Berlin Film Festival.

1960s

The next notable film production was *Lachit Borphukan* by Sarbeswar Chakraborty. Bhupen Hazarika made his musical *Shakuntala* in 1961, which proved equally successful with critics and the press, winning the president's silver medal. Following this, a chain of films went into regular production and got released, including Nip Barua's *Narakasur*, Anil Choudhury's *Matri Swarga*, Brojen Barua's *Itu Situ Bahuto* and Mukta and Anwar Hussain's *Tejimala*.

By the middle of the sixties, film began to be produced in Assam on a regular basis. However, between 1935 and 1970 a total of 62 films were produced. Besides the film makers already referred to, many others engaged in film making during the period included Pravin Sharma, Saila Barua, Amar Pathak, Indukalpa Hazarika, Brajen Barua, Dibon Barua, Debkumar Basu, Amulya Manna, Gauri Barman, Atul Bardoloi, Sujit Singha, Nalin Duara and Prafulla Barua.

1970s

During the period of 1970-82 a total of 57 Assamese films were made. New directors started emerging. Samarendra

Narayan Dev's *Aranya* (1970), Kamal Choudhury's *Bhaity* (1972, the first colour film of Assam), Manoranjan Sur's *Uttaran* (1973), Prabin Bora's *Parinam* (1974), Deuti Barua's *Bristi* (1974), Pulok Gogoi's *Khoj* (1974), Padum Barua's *Gonga Silonir Pakhi* (1976), Bhabendranath Saikia's *Sandhya Raag* (1977) and Atul Bordoloi's *Kollol* (1978) are films worth mentioning.

1980s

Notable directors of contemporary Assamese cinema are Jahnu Barua (who directed *Aparoopa*, *Papori*, *Halodhia Choraye Baodhan Khai*, *Bonani*, *Firingoti* and *Xagoroloi Bohu Door*); Sanjeev Hazarika (*Haladhar*, *Meemanxa*) and Bhabendra Nath Saikia who directed *Sandhya Raag*, *Anirbaan*, *Agnisnaan*, *Sarothi*, *Kolahol*, *Abartan*, *Itihaas* and *Kaal Sandhya*). Other directors include Santwana Bordoloi who directed *Adajya*, Bidyut Chakraborty who made *Rag Birag*, both of which have won national and international awards, and Manju Borah with her multiple award-winning films such as Baibhab, Akashitarar Kathare, and Laaz.

Halodhia Choraye Baodhan Khai became the first Assamese film to won the National Film Award for Best Feature Film in 1988 and also won multiple awards at the Locarno International Film Festival in 1988.

2000s

In the starting of the 2000s, the director-actor-musician trio of Munin Barua, Jatin Bora and Zubeen Garg made many popular hit films like *Hiya Diya Niya* and *Nayak*.

2010s

Assamese feature films certified and released in 2010s

Year	Certified	Released
2010	4	3
2011	7	6
2012	11	10
2013	15	14

2014	21	18
2015	19	8
2016	20	17
2017	16	24

The 2010s saw the release of two Assamese blockbusters - *Raamdhenu* and *Mission China*, each collecting over 1 crore in the box office. *Tumi Aahibane* and *Priyaar Priyo* became the third and fourth film respectively to cross the one crore mark while *Doordarshan Eti Jantra* have almost reached the one crore mark.

The 2010s also saw the loss of many prominent personalities like director Munin Baruah, actor Biju Phukan, musician Bhupen Hazarika, who have played an important role in shaping Assamese cinema.

2018

In 2018, *Village Rockstars* won the Best Feature Film 'Swarna Kamal' award at the 65th National Film Awards in Delhi, hence becoming the second Assamese film after *Halodhia Choraye Baodhan Khai* to won this award. The film also won awards in the categories of Best Child Artist, Best Audiography and Best Editing. The film is also selected for India's official entry to 91st Academy Awards making it the first film from Assam to do this.

On 28 July, 2018, another Assamese film *Xhoixobote Dhemalite* received three awards for Best Film, Best Actress and Best Music in 3rd Love International Film Festival in Los Angeles, US. The film also got 8 nominations. It also became the first Assamese film to release in the US.

BOHAG BIHU

Bohag Bihu or Rongali Bihu also called *Xaat Bihu* (seven Bihus) is a festival celebrated in the state of Assam and north eastern India, and marks the beginning of the Assamese New Year. It usually falls on 2 April week, historically signifying the time of harvest. It falls on 14 April in 2016 ... It unites the population of Assam regardless of their religions or backgrounds and promotes the celebration of diversity. In India it is celebrated seven days after *Vishuva Sankranti* of the month of Vaisakh or locally 'Bohag' (Bhaskar Calendar). The three primary types of Bihu are Bohag Bihu or Rongali Bihu, Kati Bihu or Kongali Bihu, and Magh Bihu or Bhogali Bihu. Each festival historically recognizes a different agricultural cycle of the paddy crops. During Rangali Bihu there are 7 pinnacle phases: 'Chot', 'Raati', 'Goru', 'Manuh', 'Kutum', 'Mela' and 'Chera'......

Raati Bihu : This phase begins on the first night of month of Chot and lasts till *Uruka.* This phase was usually performed beneath an ancient tree or in an open field illuminated by burning torches. It was celebrated in the *Chowdang* villages and was meant as a gathering for the local women. The participation of men was mostly ceremonial where they played a *pepa* i.e. a buffalo hornpipe. Another notable musical instrument played in this phase was the *bholuka baanhor toka* which is a split bamboo musical instrument.

Chot Bihu : Also called *Bali Husori*, this phase begins on the second day of the month of Chot Mah. On this day Bihu songs and dances are organized by the young at outdoor locations, fields or a *naamghor bakori* (yard of community prayer hall) till the occurrence of *Uruka*, the formal beginning of Rongali Bihu.

A bihu dancer with Japi (Assamese headgear)

1. Goru Bihu : This phase is related to the agricultural roots of Assam and the reverence of livestock which provided

an ancient method of livelihood. On the last date of Chot month or the day of *Sankranti*, the first day of Rongali Bihu is dedicated to the caring upkeep of livestock and a cattle show. Typically the collective cattle of a village are brought to a water source like a pond or a river. The cattle are washed with a combination of symbolic herbs : *maah-halodhi* (black gram and turmeric paste), whipped *dighloti* (*litsea salicifolia*, a plant with long leaf), *makhioti* (flemingia strobilifera, " tonglati "a plant with flower like soft plastic butter-fly) and pieces of *lau* (bottle gourd) and *bengena* (brinjal). People sing the following passage: "*Dighloti dighal paat, maakhi marru jaat jaat; lau khaa bengena khaa, bosore bosore bardhi jaa, maare xaru baapere xoru toi hobi bor bor goru*" . This is roughly translated as : "With our herbs and the leaves of dighloti, we drive away the flies which disturb you; we hope you accept our offering of brinjals and gourds, and continue to grow every year; and may you outgrow your parents". After washing the cattle, the remaining branches of *dighloti-makhioti and lau-bengena chat* etc. are hung on the roof of the cattle ranch signifying their participation. Games are organised which include collecting *exho ebidh haak* (101 types of vegetables), with variations of activities which may include specifics like gathering *amlori tup* (larvae of weaver ant, Oecophylla smaragdina), binding betel leaf plants, planting some bamboo roots, and many other symbolic harvest related ritual materials. There is also an occasional food fight, also known as *Kori Khel, Paakha Khel and koni-juj*. At Dusk, the cattle are paraded back to their ranches. The cattle are decorated with new harnesses, dressed in garlands, and are fed *pitha* (the typical Assamese confectionery). The day's end is marked by burning rice bran to create smoke.

2. Manuh Bihu :The first day of the Vaisakh month marks *Manuh Bihu* ('Manuh' symbolises "Elders"). . People have a special *maah halodhi* bath, put on new clothes and light *chaki* at *Gohai Ghor* (the household prayer place). "Manuh

Bihu" involves the tradition of seeking blessings from the elders in a family and presenting the ceremonial patch of *Bihuwan* or the *Gamusa* cloth, as a gift, to be worn as a symbol of cultural pride. A 'Gamusa' is an indispensable part of Assamese life and culture with its distinctive symbolic significance. The intricacy of its handcrafting symbolically historically heralded of the ideas of friendship, love, regards, warmth, hospitality and it is intimately woven into the social fabric of Assam.

3. Kutum Bihu : The second date of Visakh is *Kutum Bihu* ("Kutum" symbolises "Kin"). On this day people visit their families, relatives and friends and have lunch or dinner together and share news and stories.
4. Mela Bihu (মেলা বিহু) : The third day of Bihu is marked by the celebration of Bihu with cultural events and competitions in outdoor locales (Mela symbolises "Fair"). In the ancient days, the King and his staff used to come out to such fairs or *bihutolis* to mingle in the Bihu celebrations. This tradition of events is continued till date with *Bihu Melas*or Bihu functions. The fairs are attended by people from all over Assam and are aimed at fostering an atmosphere of the communal brotherhood and the inclusion of everyone.
5. Chera Bihu : Also called *Bohagi Bidai, Phato Bihu* it is the fourth and final day of Rongali Bihu. In different regions of Assam, people celebrate it differently but the common theme is wrapping up the celebrations with contemplation and future resolutions. It is marked by the exchange of *Pithas* made by different families during the Bihu week among their friends and relatives.

FOLK DANCES OF ASSAM

Folk dances of Assam, include the Bihu dance *and the* Bagurumba *(both danced during festivals held in the spring), the* Bhortal *dance, the* Ojapali *dance etc. Assam is home to many groups: Mongoloid, Indo-Burmese, Indo-Iranian, Aryan, Rabha, Bodo, Kachari, Karbi, Mising, Sonowal Kacharis, Mishimi and Tiwa (Lalung). These cultures come together to create an Assamese culture. Residents of the state of Assam are known as "Axomiya" (Assamese). Most tribes have their own language, although Assamese is the primary language of the state.*

Many fairs and festivals are held in Assam. Nearly all tribal festivals are held in spring and celebrate cultivation or harvest. Among festivals in Assam, the Bihu is most noteworthy; it brings together all Assamese people, regardless of background.

Bihu dance

Although the origins of Bihu dance are unknown, the first official record of it is said to be when the Ahom king Rudra Singha invited Bihu dancers to perform at the Rang Ghar fields in about 1694 for the *Rongali Bihu*.

Description

The Bihu is a group dance in which males and females dance together, but maintain separate gender roles. In general, females follow stricter line or circle formations. The male dancers and musicians enter the dancing area first, maintain their lines and follow synchronized patterns. When the female dancers enter, the male dancers break up their lines to mingle with the female dancers (who maintain their stricter formation and the order of the dance). It is usually characterized by specific postures: movements of the hips, arms and wrists; twirls, squats and bends. Male and female dance movements are very similar, with only subtle differences.

Performance

The dance is performed to traditional Bihu music. The most important musicians are the drummers (*dhulia*), who play a twin-faced drum (the *dhol*, which is hung from the neck) with one stick and a palm. There are usually more than one *dhulia* in a performance; each plays different rhythms at different sections of the performance. These rhythmic compositions, called *seus*, are traditionally formal. Before entering the dancing area, the drummers play a short and brisk rhythm. The *seu* is changed, and the drummers usually enter the dance area in line. The *mohor xingor pepa* is played (usually at the beginning) by a single player, who lays out an initial plaintive motif which sets the mood for the dance.

The male dancers then enter the area in formation and perform (accompanied by singing, in which all participate). Other instruments which accompany this dance are the *taal*, a type of cymbal; the *gogona*, a reed-and-bamboo instrument; the *toka*, a bamboo clapper and the *xutuli*, a clay whistle. Bamboo flutes are also often used.

The songs (*bihu geet*) accompanying the dance have been handed down for generations. Subjects of the lyrics include welcoming the Assamese new year, describing the life of a farmer, history and satire. Although males and females perform Bihu dance, the female Bihu dance has more variations (including freehand, twisting, with a rhythmic *pepa*, with a *kahi* (disk) and with *jaapi*—Assamese headgear). The performance may be long, but is enlivened by rapid changes in rhythm, mood, movements, pace and improvisation. Dancers and musicians are given opportunities to showcase their talents.

Types

The dance takes several forms in the different northeastern Indian groups (e.g. the Deori Bihu dance, Mising Bihu dance or Rati Bihu celebrated by Morans). However, the underlying goal of the dance remains the same: to express the desire to feel both pain and happiness.

Bagurumba

Bagurumba is a folk dance in Assam which is performed by the Bodos. It is the usually practiced during Bwisagu, a Bodo festival in the Vishuva Sankranti (mid-April). *Bwisagu* begins with cow worship; then, young people reverentially bow down to their parents and elders.

After that, Bathow is worshiped by offering the deity chicken and *zou* (rice beer). Bodo women wearing colourful *dokhna* and *aronai* perform the Bagurumba dance (also known as the Bardwisikhla dance). It is accompanied by instruments such as the *serja* (a bowed instrument), *sifung* (flute), *tharkha* (split bamboo), *kham* or *madal* (long drum, made of wood and goatskin). The festival ends with a community prayer at Garjasali. This dance is performed in the Bodo-inhabited areas of Udalguri, Kokrajhar, Baksa, Chirang, Bongaigaon, Nalbari, Darrang and Sonitpur Districts.

Bagurumba performed by Bodo girls

Bhortal Dance

Bhortal Nritya is known to have developed by Narahari Burha Bhakat. He was a well-known Satriya artist. This Bhortal Nritya of Barpeta district is said to have derived from the classical dance form of the state. This is one of the most popular dances in the state of Assam.

Performance— this dance is performed in a group. Six or seven dancers generally present the Bhortal dance of Assam together. This dance can be performed in larger groups as well. It is performed to a very fast beat. This beat is known as ' 7hiya Nom'. The dancers are equipped with cymbals while performing this dance. The use of the cymbals makes the dance presentation appear very colorful. The dance movements are designed as such that they can produce some very colorful patters. This is the uniqueness of this dance from Assam.

Bhortal Dance

Jhumair Dance

Jhumair is a traditional dance form of "Adivasi" or Tea tribes community of Assam. The dance is performed by young girls and boys together. The male members wear long traditional dresses and keep the rhythm with few traditional musical instruments, generally a Dhol or Mandar, hung on shoulders, a flute and a pair of "Taal" (two metallic discs). The girls mostly perform the dancing part, holding each other's waist and moving hands and legs forward and backward synchronously. The dance has a huge following in the "Tea tribe" dominated districts of Assam, like Udalguri, Sonitpur, Golaghat, Jorhat, Sivasagar, Dibrugarh and Tinsukia .

ASSAMESE CUISINE

Assamese cuisine is the cuisine of Assam. It is a style of cooking that is a confluence of cooking habits of the hills that favor fermentation and drying as forms of preservation and those from the plains that provide fresh vegetables and an abundance of fish and meat. Both are centered on the main ingredient — rice. The confluence of varied cultural influences in the Assam Valley has led to the staggering variety and flavours in the Assamese food. It is characterised by the use of an extremely wide variety of plant as well as animal products, owing to their abundance in the region. It is a mixture of indigenous styles with considerable regional variations and some external influences.

The cuisine is characterized by very little use of spices, little cooking over fire and strong flavors due mainly to the use of endemic exotic fruits and vegetables that are either fresh, dried or fermented. Fish is widely used, and birds like duck, squab etc. are very popular, which are often paired with a main vegetable or ingredient. Preparations are rarely elaborate. (The practice of bhuna, the gentle frying of spices before the addition of the main ingredients so common in Indian cooking, is absent in the cuisine of Assam.) The preferred oil for cooking is the pungent mustard oil.

Assamese Thali

A traditional meal in Assam begins with a *khar*, a class of dishes named after the main ingredient, and ends with a *tenga*, a sour dish. The food is usually served in bell metal utensils made by an indigenous community called Mariya. The belief is that when food and water is served in such utensils its good for health and boost up immunity. *Tamul* (betel nut, generally raw) and *paan* generally concludes the meal.

Kosu xaak aru madhuxuleng (Colocasia with Polygonum microcephalum)

Though still obscure, this cuisine has seen wider notice in recent times. The discovery of this cuisine in the popular media continues, with the presenters yet to settle on the language and the specific distinctiveness to describe it.

Ingredients

Rice

Rice is the most important ingredient in this cuisine. The large varieties of rice found in the region has led to speculation that the grain was first domesticated in the Assam-Yunnan region. Both the indica as well as the japonica varieties are grown in Assam. The most popular class of rice is the *joha* or scented rice. As a staple, rice is eaten either steam boiled (*ukhua*) or sundried (*aaroi*). Some very fine quality of rice namely, *Karaballam* or *kauribadam* etc., are available in Assam only.

Rice is eaten as snack in many forms: roasted and ground (*xandoh*), boiled in its husk and flattened (*chira*), puffed (*akhoi*). (*kumol saul*), a preparation of rice that is precooked, dried and then husked can be simply soaked in warm water and eaten as a light meal.

Rice is a part of all meals in Assam. A traditional breakfast consists of *chira* with yogurt and jaggery. Mostly farmers eat cooked rice soaked overnight (*poita*) simply accompanied with salt, mustard oil, onions, etc. Snacks are *xandoh, kumol saul* or *bora saul*, sticky rice, which can be eaten with sweet or salty accompaniments. For other major meals, rice could be boiled, steamed or wrapped in leaves and roasted. 'Sunga Saul' is a special preparation in which (sticky) rice (*bora saul*) is cooked in bamboo hollows called 'sunga'. 'Sewa diya Bhaat' is another preparation where sticky rice is steamed over boiling water. They are generally served with meat or fish. Sticky rice is also wrapped in leaves, usually plantain leaves or *tora pat*, and dropped into boiling water to prepare 'tupula bhat'.

A special class of rice preparations, called pithas are generally made only on special occasions like the Bihu. Made usually with soaked and ground glutinous rice (bora saul), they could be fried in oil with a sesame filling (*xutuli pitha*), roasted in young green bamboo over a slow fire (sunga pitha) or baked and rolled over a hot plate with a filling (*kholasaporia pitha*).

Fish

The next most important ingredient is fish, harvested from the many rivers, ponds and lakes in the region. The extremely wet climate and the large numbers of water bodies has ensured that large varieties of fresh water fish are available in abundance in the valley. It is a staple item in the Assamese palate. There is no traditional ethnic community in Assam that does not eat fish. Most traditional rural households have their own ponds for pisciculture. Some of the most popular big fishes are the *Borali* (freshwater dhark), *rou*, and *cital* (big), *khoria* (medium) (Chitala chitala), *maagur*, Xingi, *borali, bhokua* or *bahu, Xaal, Xol*, etc. The small varieties of fish available and eaten in Assam like *puthi, Ari*(long-whiskered catfish), *Goroi* (green snake head/ spotted snake head), *Koi* or *Kawoi* (climbing perch *Anabas testudineus*), *Kholihona*(Indian paradise fish *Ctenops nobilis*) *borolia, mua, ceniputhi, tengera, lachin, bhangun, pabho*, etc. The discerning gourmet can tell which region of Assam is known for which variety of fish. The *mas tenga* (sour fish), which is commonly eaten by most communities of Assam, has lately turned into a signature dish of Assamese cuisine. The most popular souring agent for the *tenga* is tomatoes, though ones made with *kajinemu* juice (thick skinned elongated lemon) and *thekera* (dried mangosteen,) are also popular.

The most common way of eating fish in traditional Assamese homes is by preparing a stew with herbs, vegetables and greens as per preference and availability. Fish is also prepared by roasting or char grilling. A favorite is small fish roasted in banana leaves (*paatotdia*). *Hukoti* is a special fish dish prepared from dried small fish like (*puthi maas*) pounded with arum stem and dried and stored in bamboo tubes. Variations of this exist among the ethnic communities of northeast India in general and Assam in particular. Dried and fermented small fish *puthy mas* (Ticto barb), three to four in number, are roasted with lavish amounts of green chilis, tomatoes, ginger and garlic (all roasted). The ingredients are then pounded in a mortar to make a coarse paste and served with rice. Fish eggs and innards are also cooked and consumed.

Meat

The Assamese meat and fish dishes are characterized by low amount of spices and oil, higher quantity of ginger, noroxinghow paat (curry leaves), Khorisa (fermented bamboo shoot) and lemon juice, and differ completely in taste from the dishes of neighbouring Bengal. Local Chicken, Venison, Squab, Mutton, Duck and Pork is very popular among the indigenous ethnic tribal Assamese communities like Sonowals, Bodo, Rabha, etc. Upper caste Assamese Hindus, such as Assamese Brahmins(including Ganaks) and Kayasthas of Assam, Kalitas of Lower Assam refrain from pork consumption. Beef is occasionally consumed by Assamese Muslims, although they traditionally refrain from consuming pork. The Christians, many ethnic communities, and the non religious sections consume all types of meat.

The basic cooking methods include cooking, shallow and deep frying. *Onla*, of the Bodos, is made with ground rice and special herbs and constitutes a complete meal in itself. Other meats include squab, duck, chicken, goat meat, venison, and turtle although venison and turtlemeat are legally prohibited. The combination of duck/white gourd and squab/papaya or banana flower is very popular. Meat is generally stewed using limited spices as well as a choice of herbs and vegetables.

Most communities of Assam are entomophagous. Ethnic tribes of certain areas partake of silkworm, water bugs, grasshoppers, and other insects. Insects are fried or cooked or roasted in leaves and then prepared according to the timing of the meal. The red ant egg is considered a delicacy during the Rongali Bihu festival.

Greens and vegetables

The environs of Assam are rich in vegetation, and green leafy vegetables, called *xaak*, are an important part of the cuisine. Some of them are grown while others like the *dhekia*(fern) grows wild. There is a bewildering variety that is eaten and according to custom, one has to have 101 different *xaak* (greens) during Rongali Bihu. Herbs, greens and vegetables are commonly eaten by simply cooking in water and salt, lightly frying, as a thick soup or by adding to varieties of lentils. They are also prepared in combination with fish, meat and eggs.

Spices

Among spices there are ginger, garlic, onion, cumin seed, black cumin, black pepper, chilli, turmeric, coriander seed, cinnamon, cardamom, clove, fenugreek seed, white mustardseed, aniseed, Malabar leaf, Cumin, etc. Some herbs peculiar to Assam are *maan dhaniya, moran Ada, madhuhulong, bhedai lota, manimuni, masundari* etc. An Assamese meal is incomplete without green chilis, many varieties of which are available in the region. Assam is famous for the bhut jolokia or *ghost pepper* which was recognized as the hottest chili in the world. *Panch-furan (mixture of 5 spices)* is used for adding flavour to Dal.

Preparations

Although modern cuisine of Assam has been influenced by east and north Indian cuisine, Assam is still rich in traditional dishes.

Khar

The khar is a signature class of preparations made with a key ingredient, also called khar. The traditional ingredient is made by filtering water through the ashes of the sun-dried skin of a few varieties of banana , which is then called *kola khar* (The name derived from the local term for banana, "kol" or "kola.") A traditional meal invariably begins with a *khar* dish, which can be prepared with raw papaya, mustard leaves, vegetables, pulses, fish or any other main ingredient.

Xôkôta is a severely bitter type of preparation. It is prepared with dry jute leaf, urad bean and *khar*. However, the combination of *khar*(alkaline) and *tenga* (acidic) is not recommended. The liquid khar is also simply eaten as *kharoli* with rice which is prepared by adding a few drops of mustard oil. Assamese people have a peculiar tradition of eating a large variety of bitter dishes, many of which are considered delicacies. Some dishes in this category include, *fresh bamboo shoot*, cooked or lightly fried, *cane shoot*, Neem leaves fried, *titabhekuri*, bitter gourd, *Xukuta*, *Titaphool*, *Sewali Phool* etc.

Masor Tenga

The *masor tenga* is a light and sour fish dish, another signature class of preparations. There are numerous ways of preparing the sour fish curry among Assamese people. The souring ingredient could be mangosteen, lemon, etc., but the most popular is made with tomatoes. Fish dishes made with fermented bamboo shoot (khorisa) are generally sour, but they are not called *tenga*. Fish is fried in mustard oil or stewed with bottle gourd or spinach. Another *tenga* dish is prepared with *matimah* (urad bean) and *outenga* (elephant apple). Bottle gourdcan be added to it. *Tengamora* or *noltenga* and lentil is a distinct *tenga* curry.

Narasingh Masor Jhol

The *narasingh masor jhol* is another authentic dish from Assam.The fishes are cooked in a light gravy of curry leaves which is a common aromatic herb used in southern and some northern parts of India. The curry leaves are also known as noro-shingho paat in Assamese. The fish preparations in Assam emphasize on retaining the natural flavors of the fishes and hence few spices are used.

Pura

Pura refers to various forms of grilled and roasted food. Vegetables, meat and fish are often served in this form. Aalu bengena pura pitika, pura maas pitika (mashed grilled fish), pura mankho etc. are a few of the popular dishes.

Poitabhat

Poitabhat is a favourite dish in Assam during the summer season. Cooked rice is soaked overnight and left to ferment. It is and served with mustard oil, onion, chili, pickles, *pitika* (mashes), etc. The 'poitabhat' preparation is sometimes made alcoholic according to preference.

Pitika

Side dishes called *pitika* - (mashes) is a signature

characteristic of this cuisine. The most popular is *aloo pitika-* (mashed potatoes) garnished with raw onions, mustard oil, green chillies and sometimes boiled eggs. *Khorisa tenga* is mashed fermented bamboo shoot, sometimes pickled in mustard oil and spices.

Kharoli is fermented mashed mustard (*Brassica campestris* var. toria) seed to which a *khar* has been added, and *kahudi* to which an acidic agent (lemon juice, dried mangosteen) has been added. *Pitikas* are also made from roasted or steamed vegetables (tomatoes and eggplants being very popular). Small fish, asiatic pennywort, *matikaduri*, *tengamora* leaves, heartleaf, *dôrôn* (*Leucus longifolia*), etc. are roasted separately wrapped in banana leaves and mashed into 'pitika'.

Pickle

Pickles are made of mango, indian gooseberry, hog plum, Indian olive, Tamarind, star fruit, mangosteen, radish, carrot, elephant apple, Indian jujube, chili, lime, garlic, etc. Panitenga and kharoli are signature Assamese pickles made from ground mustard seeds.

Chutney and salad

Chutney is made of coriander, spinach, tomato, heartleaf, curry leaf, chilli, lentil, chickpea etc. *Xukan masor chutney* (chutney made of dried fish) is popular among the tribal communities. Salad is made of carrot, radish, tomato, cucumber, beetroot, etc.

Bora

'Bora' are fried balls of mashed lentil or gram — it is equivalent to vada in few other Indian languages. It may contain other green leafy vegetable locally called 'xaak' within it, and it is best while served with 'teteli' (tamarind) curry or dip. There is a huge variety of 'bora' preparations in Assamese cuisine. The base ingredients include greens, vegetables, fruits, flowers, skin, and shoots of various plants. 'Bora' can also be prepared from fish eggs etc.

Pokori *(fritter)*

Fritter is made of flower and tender leaves of pumpkin, banana, tender leaves of bottle gourd, eggplant, tender leaves of night-flowering jasmine, etc.

Some other preparations

Some other preparations in Assamese cuisine include *Kahudi*, *Panitenga*, *Khorikatdiya*, *Tenga sorsoriya*, *Posola*, etc.

Snacks and cakes

Jolpan

Jolpan (snacks) in Assamese is what is breakfast although it is not always served as breakfast in Assamese cuisine. They are eaten as light meals between main meals and widely served during Bihu, weddings, Assamese *shraadh*s or any other kind of special occasions and gatherings. Some types of jolpan are *Bora saul* (varieties of sticky rice), *Komal Saul*, *Xandoh*, *Chira*, *Muri*, *Akhoi*, Sunga saul, etc. eaten in combination with hot milk, curd, jaggery, yogurt or seasonal ripe fruits. These are probably some of the earliest forms of "cereals". Assamese people have been eating them mainly as breakfast for many centuries.

Pitha

Pitha (rice cake) is a special class of rice preparation generally made only on occasions like Bihu in Assam. Made usually with soaked and ground rice, they could be fried in oil, roasted over a slow fire or baked and rolled over a hot plate. Some pithas are *Til Pitha*, *Ghila Pitha*, *Xutuli Pitha*, *Sunga Pitha*, *Bhapotdiya Pitha*, *Lakhimi Pitha*, *Tora Pitha*, *Tekeli Pitha*, *Deksi Pitha*, *Muthiya Pitha*, *Kholasapori Pitha*, etc.

It is made in other areas such as West Bengal, Maharashtra, Orissa (Odhisa), Delhi, Punjab, etc.

Laru

Larus are sweet balls that are associated with traditional

Assamese food: *Laskara*, narikolor laru, *tilor laru* are often seen in Assamese cuisine.

Tea

Tea (*Saah* in Assamese) is an indispensable part of Assamese cuisine. It is served in form of Black tea, Milk tea, Spiced tea, Green Tea, Lemon tea (adding lemon juice to black tea), etc.

Some other snacks

Some other snacks include roti, luchi, and ghugni.

SYMBOLS

Symbolism is an ancient cultural practice in Assam and is still a very important part of Assamese way of life. Various elements are being used to represent beliefs, feelings, pride, identity, etc.

Tamulpan, *Xorai* and *Gamosa* are three important symbolic elements in Assamese culture. *Tamulpan*(the areca nut and betel leaves) or *guapan* (gua from *kwa*) are considered along with the Gamosa (a typical woven cotton or silk cloth with embroidery) as the offers of devotion, respect and friendship. The Tamulpan-tradition is an ancient one and is being followed since time-immemorial with roots in the aboriginal Austro-Asiatic culture. *Xorai* is a traditionally manufactured bell-metal article of great respect and is used as a container-medium while performing respectful offers. Moreover, symbolically many ethno-cultural groups use specific clothes to portray respect and pride.

There were many other symbolic elements and designs, but are now only found in literature, art, sculpture, architecture, etc. or in use today for only religious purposes. The typical designs of *assamese-lion*, *dragon*, *flying-lion*(Hindi-udta sher), etc. were used for symbolising various purposes and occasions.

The archaeological sites such as the Madan Kamdev (c. 9th–10th centuries AD) exhibits mass-scale use of lions, dragon-lions and many other figures of demons to show case power and prosperity. The Vaishnava monasteries and many other architectural sites of late medieval period display the use of lions and dragons for symbolic effects.

Festivals and traditions

A Bihu dancer blowing a **pepa** *(horn)*

There are diversified important traditional festivals in Assam. Bihu is the most important and common and celebrated all over Assam. It is the Assamese new year celebrated in April of the Gregorian calendar. Durga Puja is another festival celebrated with great enthusiasm. Muslims celebrate two Eids (Eid ul-Fitr and Eid al-Adha) with much eagerness all over Assam.

Bihu is a series of three prominent festivals. Primarily a non-religious festival celebrated to mark the seasons and the significant points of a cultivator's life over a yearly cycle. Three Bihus, *rongali* or *bohag*, celebrated with the coming of spring and the beginning of the sowing season; *kongali* or *kati*, the barren bihu when the fields are lush but the barns are empty; and the *bhogali* or *magh*, the thanksgiving when the crops have been harvested and the barns are full.

Bihu songs and Bihu dance are associated to *rongali* bihu. The day before the each bihu is known as 'uruka'. The first day of 'rongali bihu' is called 'Goru bihu' (the bihu of the cows), when the cows are taken to the nearby rivers or ponds to be bathed with special care. In recent times the form and nature of celebration has changed with the growth of urban centres.

Bwisagu is one of the popular seasonal festivals of the Bodos. Bwisagu start of the new year or age. Baisagu is a Boro word which originated from the word "Baisa" which means year or age, ang "Agu" that means starting or start.

Bushu Dima or simply Bushu is a major harvest festival of the Dimasa people. This festival is celebrated during the end of January. Officially 27 January has been declared as the day of Bushu Dima festival. The Dimasa people celebrate their festival by playing musical instruments- khram (a type of drum), muri (a kind of huge long flute). The people dances to the different tunes called "murithai" and each dance has got its name, the prominent being the "Baidima" There are three types of Bushu celebrated among the Dimasas Jidap, Surem and Hangsou.

Moreover, there are other important traditional festivals being celebrated every year on different occasions at different places. Many of these are celebrated by different ethno-cultural groups (sub and sister cultures). Some of these are:

- Me-Dam-Me-Phi
- Ali-Aye-Ligang
- Rongker
- Kherai
- Garja
- Bisu (Deori)
- Awnkham Gwrlwi Janai
- Chojun/Swarak
- Deusi Bhailo (Traditional Nepalese songs that are sung during the festival of light " Dipavali *and also called "Tihar")*
- Sokk-erroi
- Hacha-kekan
- Hapsa Hatarnai

- Porag
- Bathow
- Wangala
- Bohuwa dance

Other few yearly celebrations are Doul Utsav of Barpeta, Brahmaputra Beach Festival, Guwahati, Kaziranga Elephant Festival, Kaziranga and Dehing Patkai Festival, Lekhapani, Karbi Youth Festival of Diphu and International Jatinga Festival, Jatinga can not be forgotten. Few yearly *Mela's* like Jonbeel Mela, began in the 15th century by the Ahom Kings, Ambubachi Mela, Guwahati etc.

Lachit Divas' is celebrated to promote the ideals of Lachit Borphukan – the legendary general of Assam's history. Sarbananda Sonowal, the chief minister of Assam took part in the Lachit Divas celebration at the statue of Lachit Borphukan at Brahmaputra riverfront on 24 November 2017. He said, the first countrywide celebration of 'Lachit Divas' would take place in New Delhi followed by state capitals such as Hyderabad, Bangalore and Kolkata in a phased manner.

Music, dance, and drama

Performing arts include: *Ankia Naat* (*Onkeeya Naat*), a traditional Vaishnav dance-drama (*Bhaona*) popular since the 15th century AD. It makes use of large masks of gods, goddesses, demons and animals and in between the plays a *Sutradhar* (*Xutrodhar*) continues to narrate the story.

Besides Bihu dance and *Huchory* performed during the *Bohag Bihu*, dance forms of tribal minorities such as; *Kushan nritra* of Rajbongshi's, *Bagurumba* and *Bordoicikhla* dance of Bodos, Mishing Bihu, *Banjar Kekan* performed during *Chomangkan* by Karbis, Jhumair of Tea tribes are some of the major folk dances. *Sattriya* (*Sotriya*) dance related to Vaishnav tradition is a classical form of dance. Moreover, there are several other age-old dance-forms such as Barpeta's *Bhortal Nritya*, *Deodhoni Nritya*, *Ojapali*, *Beula Dance*, *Ka Shad Inglong Kardom*, *Nimso Kerung*, etc. The tradition of modern moving theatres is typical of Assam with immense popularity of many large theatre groups such as Kohinoor, Sankardev, Abahan, Bhagyadevi, Hengul, Brindabon, Itihas etc.

The indigenous folk music has influenced the growth of a modern idiom, that finds expression in the music of artists like Jyoti Prasad Agarwala, Bishnuprasad Rabha, Parvati Prasad Baruwa, Bhupen Hazarika, Pratima Barua Pandey, Anima Choudhury, Luit Konwar Rudra Baruah, Jayanta Hazarika, Khagen Mahanta, Deepali Borthakur, *Ganashilpi* Dilip Sarma, Sudakshina Sarma among many others. Among the new generation, Zubeen Garg, Jitul Sonowal, Angaraag Mahanta and Joi Barua. There is an award given in the honour of Bishnuprasad Rabha for achievements in the cultural/music world of Assam by the State Government.

Cuisine

Assamese Thali

Typically, an Assamese meal consists of many things such as *bhat* (rice) with *dal* (lentils), *masoor jool* (fish curry), with *mangxô* (meat curry) or *xaak* and *bhaji* (herbs and vegetables).

Rice is one of the main dishes of Assam, and a variety of different rices are grown and eaten in different ways: roasted, grounded, boiled or just soaked.

Fish curries made of free range wild fish as well as *Bôralí*, *rôu*, *illish*, or *sitôl* are the most popular. Fowl such as ducks and pigeon are used in dishes while pork(by tribals), chicken and mutton dishes are mainly popular among the younger generation.

Another favourite combination is *luchi* (fried flatbread), a curry which can be vegetarian or non-vegetarian, and *asar* (pickle).

The two main characteristics of a traditional meal in Assam are *khar* (an Alkali, named after its main ingredient) and the sour dish *tenga*. *Khorika* is the smoked or fired meat eaten with the meal. The various meats more commonly taken include mutton, fowl, duck/goose, fish, pigeon, beef and pork(among Muslim, Christian and tribal communities respectively) ; these being often involved with religious ceremonies. Other kinds of meat include grasshoppers, locusts, silkworms, snails, eels, wild fowl and other birds, deer meat and so on.

Khorisa (fermented bamboo shoots) are used at times to flavour curries while they can also be preserved and made into pickles. *Koldil* (banana flower) and squash can be cooked into *sabji's*.

Many tribal households still continue to brew their traditional drinks; variously known as Laupani, Xaaj, Paniyo, Jou, Joumai, Hor, Apang, and so on. During the time of the traditional festivities, guests are offered these drinks. Declining then is considered socially offensive.

The food is often served in bell metal dishes and platters like *Knahi*, *Maihang* and so on.

Literature

Most literary works are written in Assamese although other local language such as Boro and Dimasa are also represented. In the 19th and 20th century, Assamese and other literature was modernised by authors including Lakshminath Bezbaroa, Birinchi Kumar Barua, Hem Barua, Dr. Mamoni Raisom Goswami, Bhabendra Nath Saikia, Birendra Kumar Bhattacharya, Hiren Bhattacharyya, Homen Borgohain, Bhabananda Deka, Rebati Mohan Dutta Choudhury, Mahim Bora, Lal Bahadur Chettri, Syed Abdul Malik, Surendranath Medhi, Hiren Gohain etc.

Fine arts

The archaic Mauryan Stupas discovered in and around Goalpara district are the earliest examples (c. 300 BC to c. 100 AD) of ancient art and architectural works. The remains discovered in Daparvatiya (*Doporboteeya*) archaeological site with a beautiful doorframe in Tezpur are identified as the best examples of art works in ancient Assam with influence of SarnathSchool of Art of the late Gupta period.

Painting is an ancient tradition of Assam. Xuanzang (7th century AD) mentions that among the Kamarupa king Bhaskaravarma's gifts to Harshavardhana there were paintings and painted objects, some of which were on Assamese silk. Many of the manuscripts such as Hastividyarnava (A Treatise on Elephants), the *Chitra Bhagawata* and in the Gita Govinda from the Middle Ages bear excellent examples of traditional paintings.

Traditional crafts

Bell metal made sorai and sophura are important parts of culture

Assam has a rich tradition of crafts;, Cane and bamboo craft, bell metal and brass craft, silk and cotton weaving, toy and mask making, pottery and terracotta work, wood craft, jewellery making, and musical instruments making have remained as major traditions.

Cane and bamboo craft provide the most commonly used utilities in daily life, ranging from household utilities, weaving accessories, fishing accessories, furniture, musical instruments, construction materials, etc. Utilities and symbolic articles such as *Sorai* and *Bota* made from bell metal and brass are found in every Assamese household. Hajo and Sarthebari(*Sorthebaary*) are the most important centres of traditional bell-metal and brass crafts. Assam is the home of several types of silks, the most prestigious are: Muga – the natural golden silk, Pat – a creamy-bright-silver coloured silk and Eri – a variety used for manufacturing warm clothes for winter. Apart from Sualkuchi (*Xualkuchi*), the centre for the traditional silk industry, in almost every parts of the Brahmaputra Valley, rural households produce silk and silk garments with excellent embroidery designs. Moreover, various ethno-cultural groups in Assam make different types of cotton garments with unique embroidery designs and wonderful colour combinations.

Moreover, Assam possesses unique crafts of toy and mask making mostly concentrated in the Vaishnav Monasteries, pottery and terracotta work in Western Assam districts and wood craft, iron craft, jewellery, etc. in many places across the region.

Media

Print media include Assamese dailies *Amar Asom*, *Asomiya Khobor*, *Asomiya Pratidin*, *Dainik Agradoot*, *Dainik Janambhumi*, *Dainik Asam*, *Gana Adhikar*, *Janasadharan* and *Niyomiya Barta*. *Asom Bani*, *Sadin* and *Bhal Khabar* are Assamese weekly newspapers. English dailies of Assam include *The Assam Tribune*, *The Sentinel*, *The Telegraph*, *The Times of India*,*The North East Times*, *Eastern Chronicle* and *The Hills Times*. *Thekar*, in the Karbi language has the largest circulation of any daily from Karbi Anglong district. *Bodosa* has the highest circulation of any Bodo daily from BTC. *Dainik Jugasankha* is a Bengali daily with editions from Dibrugarh, Guwahati, Silchar and Kolkata. *Dainik Samayik Prasanga*, *Dainik Prantojyoti*, *Dainik Janakantha* and *Nababarta Prasanga* are other prominent Bengali dailies published in the Barak Valley towns of Karimganj and Silchar. Hindi dailies include *Purvanchal Prahari*, *Pratah Khabar* and *Dainik Purvoday*.

Broadcasting stations of All India Radio have been established in five big cities: Dibrugarh, Guwahati, Kokrajhar, Silchar and Tezpur. Local news and music are the main priority for that station. Assam has three public service broadcasting service stations at Dibrugarh, Guwahati and Silchar. Guwahati is the headquarters of a number of electronic medias like Assam Talks, DY 365, News Live, News 18 Assam/North-East, Prag News and Pratidin Time.

ASSAM SOCIETY

One of the most beautiful states of India, Assam is the gateway to the enchanting and unexploited northeastern part of the country. With the majestic Brahmaputra river, magnificent hills and its rich flora and fauna, the state is a tourist paradise. The vibrant life style, the all-smile people, presence of diverse tribes and cultures, are the main points of the wonderful Assam Society. The history of Assam dates back to the time of the Aryans and has got its mention in the epics, the Tantric, Vedic and Buddhist Literature. The land has been ruled my great rulers of many dynasties. The people of the state are friendly and they belong to different tribes and communities.

Several religions are practiced in the state, proving its secular outlook. Some of the religions that are followed in the state are:

- Hinduism
- Buddhism
- Christianity
- Islam
- Vaishnavasim

Apart from the Assamese, the Bengali speaking population and the Nepalis also form a major portion of the state. The diverse culture of the state has brought a rich treasure of art, craft and music with it. Assam is famous for its wood, cane and bamboo crafts, pottery, handlooms, jewelry and colorful masks.

The feet tapping Bihu and Jhumur dances of the state are no more bounded by its borders but they are quite popular in all parts of the country.

Shopping

Visitors from outside the state like to collect some mementos while they return back to home. While shopping in Assam, the tourists mainly prefer to buy the arts and crafts products and the Assam tea, which is known world wide for its exotic flavor. The articles that are mostly bought by the tourists visiting Assam are the hand made items of craft. The Assamese artisans are known for their skills in art and craft for a long time. The craftsmen make articles from cane and bamboo and the artisans are known for their terracotta works.

Food

Food of Assam, as of any other place, is largely influenced by its climate, soil and vegetation. This north-eastern state of India is mainly of agrarian nature. Rice is the staple diet and the common people of Assam eat it everyday. Along with rice, fish curry is very common. Other dishes include those made of lentils, vegetables, meat and some sweet dishes. The people of Assam prefer to eat non - spicy foods. Spices like cumin, coriander, mustard, ginger, garlic, fenugreek, panch foran, cardamom and some ingredients that are found in Assam only are generally used.

Tribe

The population of Assam largely comprised of numerous Assam Tribes with their varied customs and beliefs. Starting from the plains to the hilly areas, the land of Assam is inhabited by different tribes. Some of the prominent tribes of Assam are:

- Bodo
- Singpho
- Santhal
- Dimasa people

- Karbi
- Khamti
- Khamyang
- Mishing
- Nishi
- Phake
- Rabha

People

Keeping in sync with the picturesque landscapes and colorful customs, the Assam People are a perfect example of unity in diversity. Consisting mostly of numerous tribes, the people of Assam practice different religions and customs. There are people from all parts of the country residing in the state with a prominence of Bengali speaking community and the Nepalis.

The Bodos are the most prominent mongoloid tribe of the state. Some sections of the Bodos have also demanded a separate state for themselves – the Bodoland, which has resulted in insurgency in the state. The Santhals are one of the oldest tribes of east India. They are good soldiers and proud of their race. The Phake or the Phakial tribes are said to be having their origins in Thailand.

Music

Assam Music is derived from the ancient folklores of the tribal communities that inhabit various corners of the state from a long time. Bihugeet is one of the oldest forms of Assamese music which is sung by people during the famous festival of Bihu. Bharigaan, Bargeet, Ojapali and Jhumur are some other music variations of Assam.

Some of the popular forms of Assam Music that are all-pervasive in the state are:

- Folk Music
- Regional Folk Music
- Ethnic

- Bihugeet
- Allied Styles
- Bhakti Music

Dance

There are various styles of Assam Dance. The most famous among these dance forms of Assam is the Bihu dance. It is a folk genre and is performed during the spring festival of Bihu. Apart from the Bihu there are many other folk and devotional dance forms in the state. Most of the folk dances of Assam are performed by both men and women. They are accompanied by lively music.

The various forms of Assam Dance:

- Bihu
- Satriya Nritya
- Jumur Dance
- Barpeta's bhortal Nritya
- Folk

Art & Culture

The Culture of Assam is often referred to as hybrid culture. It has developed by the gradual assimilation of cultures and traditions of various ethno-cultural groups. Assamese culture is closely associated with some of the major elements like festivals, dance, music, paintings and traditional crafts. Assam is a treasure trove of cultural potpourri. Assam art is renowned all across the country for its skilled craftsmanship and variety and techniques. Be it the exquisite traditional Muga and Vaishavite silks or the bamboo and cane artifacts, Assam is the master of it all.

Craft

Representing the rich cultural heritage and traditional legacy of Assam, the craft of Assam portrays the artistic mastery of the local craftsmen. The beautiful artifacts of the state, has captured the imagination of the world. Assam is known all over the world for its exclusive craft work that draws the attention of every individual. The traditional knowledge of creating beautiful pieces of art and craft work has triggered down to the modern era. The exclusive pieces of art and craft work of Assam are equipped with excellent infrastructural facilities and support from the state government.

PEOPLE OF ASSAM

The people of Assam inhabit a multi-ethnic, multi-linguistic and multi-religious society. They speak languages that belong to three main language groups: Indo-Aryan, Austroasiatic and Tibeto-Burman. The large number of ethnic and linguistic groups, the population composition and the peopling process in the state has led to it being called an "India in miniature".

Populating Assam and social formations

Geographically Assam contains fertile river valleys surrounded and interspersed by mountains and hills. It is accessible from Tibet in the north (via Bum La, Tse La, Tunga), across the Patkai in the Southeast (via Diphu, Kumjawng, Hpungan, Chaukam, Pangsau, More-Tamu) and from Burma across the Arakan Yoma (via An, Taungup). In the west both the Brahmaputra valley and the Barak valley open widely to the Gangetic plains. Assam has been populated via all these accessible points in the past. It has been estimated that there were eleven major waves and streams of ethnolinguistic migrations across these points over time.

Pre-historic

Anthropological accounts of Assam demography is marked by several waves of different racial migration. The Austric which were formed by the intermix of Australoid and Paleo-mongoloids were the first inhabitants. There are Neolithical sites present all over Northeast including Arunachal Pradesh, Sadiya, Dibrugarh, Lakhimpur, Nagaon, Naga hills, Karbi Anglong, Nagaon, Kamrup, Garo and Khasi hills of Meghalaya, etc. which shows the distribution of these early settlers. Most of these people were absorbed by the Tibeto-Burman groups who arrived about 4000–5000 years ago, while a fraction moved to the hills of Meghalaya and the other fraction moved near wetlands and rivers present across the Brahmaputra Valley. This has been repeatedly proved by DNA reports which shows the presence of Austro-asiatic genes in the Tibeto-Burman groups like Kacharis(Bodos, Dimasas, Chutias, Morans, Sonowals, Rabhas, Tiwas, Koch-Rajbongshi etc.) as well as Karbis, Nagas, etc. The Mon-khmer speakers who settled in the hills of Meghalaya are known as Khasis and Jaintias and the Keot(Kaibarta) community which resided near foothills and wetlands today.

The Tibeto-Burman speaking people arrived through the various passes in the Himalayas located in the North and the East of Assam. Today, these groups form the majority (about 60%) of Assam's population and are identified as the Kachari peoplescattered all over Assam; the Monpa and Sherdukpen peoples of Bhutan and Arunachal Pradesh; the Mishings, and Karbis of Central Assam.

There was another notable migration of a group of Dravidian people during this period . These were the group of Dravidian Nadiyals/Doms who migrated on or before the arrival of the Tibeto-Burmans. In the course of time they assimilated with various Mongoloid ethnic groups and now possess more Mongoloid physical features than Dravidian features.

Proto-historic and ancient

The third major ingress into Assam are attributed to the Indo-Aryans from North India (Wave 3) into the Brahmaputra Valley after 500 BCE (mostly during the 3rd century AD Varman rule). This signaled the dawn of the proto-historic period and this immigration continued into the ancient and Medieval periods. At the end of the ancient period (c1205), the first Muslims (Wave 4), captive soldiers of the defeated Bakhtiar Khilji, settled in the Hajo area.

Medieval

The next major immigrants were the Ahoms (Wave 5) when Sukaphaa lead his group into Assam via the Pangsau Pass in the Patkai from South China. The Ahoms were followed by other Tai peoples who were Buddhists (Wave 6): Khamti, Khamyang, Aiton, Tai Phake and Turung peoples, who settled in Upper Assam and Arunachal Pradesh. This continued well into the colonial times. At the end of the Medieval period a small contingent of Sikhs gave rise to a minuscule but prominent group.

Colonial and post-independence

In the beginning of the colonial period in Assam after the First Anglo-Burmese War and the Treaty of Yandaboo (1826), the political instability led to the immigration of Kachin and Kuki people (Wave 7) into the region across the Patkai and Arakan Yoma. They constitute the Singphos in Upper Assam, and the Kuki-Chin tribes in Karbi Anglong and Dima Hasao. The beginning of tea plantations in Assam (1835) by the British led to settlements of Mundari speaking people (Wave 8) (Munda, Santal, Savara, Oraon, Gond etc. tribes). The beginning of British administration also led to a large influx of service holders and professionals from Bengal, Rajasthan, Nepal, etc. (Wave 9). To increase land productivity, the British encouraged Muslim peasants from Mymensingh district of present-day Bangladesh (Wave 10) to settle in Assam that began in 1901. The last major group to immigrate are the Bengali Hindu refugees, especially from the Sylhet district of Bangladesh following the Partition of India (Wave 11).

Inputs from these and other smaller groups have gone towards the building of a unique multi-ethnic socio-cultural situation.

3

Government and Politics

INTRODUCTION

Assam has Governor Jagdish Mukhi as the head of the state, the unicameral Assam Legislative Assembly of 126 members, and a government led by the Chief Minister of Assam. The state is divided into five regional divisions.

Local government

As of June 2016, the state has 33 administrative districts. On 15 August 2015, five new districts were formed in addition to former 27 districts. The five new districts are Biswanath (carved out of Sonitpur), Charaideo (of Sivasagar), Hojai (of Nagaon), South Salmara-Mankachar (of Dhubri) and West Karbi Anglong (of Karbi Anglong). On 27 June 2016, Majuli declared as district (1st river island district of India). These districts are further sub-divided into 54 "Sub-divisions" or *Mahakuma*. Every district is administered from a district headquarters with the office of the Deputy Commissioner, District Magistrate, Office of the District Panchayat and usually with a district court.

The districts are delineated on the basis of the features such as the rivers, hills, forests, etc. and majority of the newly constituted districts are sub-divisions of the earlier districts.

The local governance system is organised under the *jila-parishad* (District Panchayat) for a district, *panchayat* for group of or individual rural areas and under the urban local bodies for the towns and cities.

There are now 2489 village panchayats covering 26247 villages in Assam. The 'town-committee' or *nagar-somiti* for small towns, 'municipal board' or *pouro-sobha* for medium towns and municipal corporation or *pouro-nigom* for the cities consist of the urban local bodies.

For the revenue purposes, the districts are divided into revenue circles and *mouzas*; for the development projects, the districts are divided into 219 'development-blocks' and for law and order these are divided into 206 police stations or *thana*. As on 19 May 2016, BJP under the leadership of Sarbananda Sonowal won the Assembly elections, thus forming the first BJP led government in Assam.

Guwahati is the largest metropolitan area and urban conglomeration administered under the highest form of urban local body – Guwahati Municipal Corporation in Assam. The Corporation administers an area of 216.79 km^2. All other urban centres are managed under Municipal Boards.

POLITICS OF ASSAM

The political structure of Assam in India is headed by the ceremonial post of the Governor. He is assisted by a council of ministers, headed by the Chief Minister, who are members of the Assam Assembly. In recent years the Governor has become more powerful, especially because the last two Governors have been ex-Army generals and the Army is entrusted with anti-insurgency operations against ULFA and other armed groups.

History

The Assam legislative structure is unicameral and consists of the 126-member Assam Assembly. Members are elected for a period of 5 years. The Assam Assembly is presided over by the Speaker, who is generally a member of the ruling party.

National Legislature

- Karimganj *1* – All India United Democratic Front
- Silchar *2* – Indian National Congress
- Autonomous District *3* – Indian National Congress
- Dhubri *4* – All India United Democratic Front
- Kokrajhar *5* – Independent
- Barpeta *6* – All India United Democratic Front
- Gauhati *7* – Bharatiya Janata Party
- Mangaldoi *8* – Bharatiya Janata Party
- Tezpur *9* – Bharatiya Janata Party
- Nowgong *10* – Bharatiya Janata Party
- Kaliabor *11* – Indian National Congress
- Jorhat *12* – Bharatiya Janata Party
- Dibrugarh *13* – Bharatiya Janata Party
- Lakhimpur *14* – Bharatiya Janata Party

POLITICAL PARTIES

Asom Bharatiya Janata Party

The Asom Bharatiya Janata Party is a break-away group of the Bharatiya Janata Party in Assam. Asom BJP was founded by senior BJP leader and former Inspector General of Police, Hiranya Bhattacharya in 2001. Bhattacharya had objected to the decision of BJP to align with the Asom Gana Parishad.

Asom BJP contested the 2001 state assembly polls unsuccessfully.

Asom Gana Parishad

Asom Gana Parishad (Assam Peoples Association), is a political party in Assam, India. The AGP was formed after the historic Assam Accord of 1985 when Prafulla Kumar Mahanta was elected as the youngest chief minister of the country. The AGP has formed government twice from 1985 to 1989 and from 1996 to 2001.

The party recently split, with former Chief Minister, Prafulla Kumar Mahanta, forming the Asom Gana Parishad (Progressive).

Asom Gana Parishad (Progressive)

Asom Gana Parishad (Progressive) or AGP(P) is a regional political party in Assam, India. It was formed by Prafulla Kumar Mahanta after he was expelled in 2005 by the Asom Gana Parishad for anti-party activities.

In the 2006 Assembly elections, the party won just one seat.

Asom Gana Sangram Parishad

Asom Gana Sangram Parishad (Assam Popular Struggle Association), a political party in the Indian state of Assam. AGSP was launched by the Asom Jatiyatabadi Yuva Chatra Parishad (AJYCP) in 1999. Party president is Jatindra Kumar Borgohain.

In the 2001 state legislative assembly polls in the state, AGSP joined the Rashtriya Democratic Alliance led by the Nationalist Congress Party.

Asom Jatiya Sanmilan

Asom Jatiya Sanmilan (Assam National Conference), a political party in the Indian state of Assam. AJS was founded by Asom Gana Parishad dissident Bhrigu Phukan in 1998.

In March 2001 the AJS General Secretary Hemanta Barman and many other members joined the Indian National Congress.

In the state legislative assembly elections 2001 AJS contested as a part of the Rashtriya Democratic Alliance, on a Nationalist Congress Party symbol.

Autonomous State Demand Committee

Autonomous State Demand Committee, originally the Peoples Democratic Front, was set-up as a mass organization of the Communist Party of India (Marxist-Leninist) Liberation in order to fight for statehood for the Karbi Anlong region in the Indian state Assam. Several elections to the Lok Sabha and the District Council were won under ASDC banner. Dr. Jayanta Rongpi represented the area in the Lok Sabha, elected as the ASDC candidate in 1991, 1996 and 1998.

Later a split occurred in ASDC, with one section the Autonomous State Demand Committee (United) breaking away from CPI(ML) Liberation and aligning with the Bharatiya Janata Party. The group loyal to CPI(ML) Liberation reorganized themselves as Autonomous State Demand Committee (Progressive).

Bodo People's Progressive Front

Bodo People's Progressive Front (BPPF) is a political organization in Assam formed on April 12, 2005 for participation in the BTAD elections. The party consisted of erstwhile members of ABSU and BLTF.

Split: The party suffered a vertical split with the erstwhile ABSU members forming the Rabiram Narzary fraction (BPPF(R)), and the erstwhile members of BLTF forming the Hagrama Mohilary fraction (BPPF(H)).

BPPF(H): The Hagrama fraction aligned with the INC in the April 2006 elections for the Assam Assembly and won 11 seats. It became the junior partner in the Assam government. This was a historical occasion since the Bodo's, long associated with the Bodoland statehood movement, are now sharing power in Dispur, the capital of Assam.

BPPF(R): The Rabiram fraction, aligned with the AGP in the April 2006 elections, did not win any seats in the Assam Assembly.

Cachar Congress

Cachar Congress, was a regional political party in the Barak Valley, Assam, India. CC was formed ahead of the 2001 Assam assembly elections by a group of Indian National Congress dissidents. The founders of CC were dissatisfied with the distribution of tickets for election and the leadership of Santosh

Mohan Dev. Santosh Mohan Dev is a Veteran leader of the Indian National Congress. He has been elected to parliament an unprecedented 7 times from Slichar (the political centre of Cachar), and has been a member of Parliament in all but one year since 1980 spanning 2 and a half decades of distinguished public service.

Through his political career as an elected representative S. M. Dev has held crucial cabinet posts such as minister of state for defence, tourism, communication and steel. He is currently the minister of industry in the Union Cabinet. His salient achievements include, the Deregulation of steel in the mid 1990s when he was minister of steel which unshackled potential of the indigenous steel industry making India a global powerhouse in the production of steel.

He was also instrumental in setting up a national university in Silchar Assam. He also played a key role in the freight equalisation scheme in the early 90s in India which removed unequal rail freight charges among the states, thereby making them more competitive.

The president of CC was Anil Chandra Dey.

CC contested the 2004 Lok Sabha elections.

On November 17 2004 CC merged with Bharatiya Janata Party. Sources claimed that CC had 520 members at the time of the merger

Natun Asom Gana Parishad

Natun Asom Gana Parishad, a political party in the Indian state of Assam. NAGP was formed through a split of Asom Gana Parishad (AGP). NAGP was led by Bhrigu Phukan, who had been state Home Minister of AGP 1985-1990. Phukan had been one of the principal leaders of the violent agitations of All Assam Students Union in the early 1980's.

NAGP voiced separatist demands more clearly than AGP.

In 1994 NAGP merged with AGP. Phukan, was expelled from AGP in 1997.

Plain Tribals Council of Assam

The Plain Tribals Council of Assam is a political party in the Indian state of Assam. In 1966, the PTCA launched a militant agitation for a separate tribal state called 'Udayachal'.

Rashtriya Democratic Alliance

Rashtriya Democratic Alliance (National Democratic Alliance), was a front of five political parties contesting the 2001 state legislative assembly elections in the Indian state of Assam. RDA included Nationalist Congress Party, Asom Jatiya Sanmilan, Asom Gana Sangram Parishad, Purbanchaliya Loka Parishad and Janata Dal (Secular).

RDA should not be confused with National Democratic Alliance.

Trinamool Gana Parishad

Trinamool Gana Parishad (Grassroot Peoples Association), political party in the Indian state of Assam. TGP was founded as a splinter-group of Asom Gana Parishad 2000. The party is led by Atul Bora.

In the state elections of 2001 TGP was allied with BJP.

In the Lok Sabha elections 2004 TGP put up one candidate, Deben Dutta from Guwahati. Dutta got 14 933 votes (1,69%).

United Minorities Front, Assam

United Minorities Front, Assam is a regional political party in Assam, India. UMFA was set up in 1985 by the All Assam Minority Students Union, as a response to the militant "anti-foreigner" agitations of All Assam Students Union and the signing of the Assam Accord. The support of UMFA comes mainly from Bengali Muslims.

The president of UMFA is Hafiz Rashid Ahmed Chowdhury.

United People's Party of Assam

United People's Party of Assam, a political party in the

Indian state of Assam. UPPA was an ally of Asom Gana Parishad and took part in a AGP-led government in the state. On December 17, 2000, UPPA merged with Samajwadi Party.

United Tribal Nationalist Liberation Front

United Tribal Nationalist Liberation Front, a regional political party in Assam, India. UTNLF was launched by the PTCA (Progressive) (splinter group of Plain Tribals Council of Assam) in 1984. UTNLF demands statehood for the Bodo areas.

The UTNLF led a violent campaign during the 1990s against both the Assamese and the Indian military units in the area.

4

Language and Literature

LANGUAGES

Assamese and Bodo are the major indigenous and official languages of the state while Bengali holds official status in particular districts in the Barak Valley. Traditionally Assamese was the language of the commons (of mixed origin - Bodo, Khasi, Sanskrit, Magadhan Prakrit) of the ancient kingdoms such as Kamrupa and Kamatapur in Assam.

Traces of the language can be found in many poems in Charyapada written by Luipa, Sarahapa, etc. during the period of the Xalostombho / Salastambha dynasty (7th/8th Century AD) of Kamarupa Kingdom. Modern Kamrupi dialect is the remnant of this language. Moreover, Assamese in its ancient and medieval form was used by almost every ethno-cultural group as the lingua-franca of the region. Probably the language was then required for needed economic integration and was also probably spread through the stronger and larger politico-economic systems such as that of the ancient Kamrupa. Traditional and localised forms of this language still exist in Nagaland, Arunachal Pradesh, North Bengal, Kacar (Cachar) and in Southern Assam (similarities with Chittagonian language in present-day Bangladesh exists).

The form used in the upper Assam was enriched by contributions from many eastern immigrations such as of those of Tai-Ahoms and others beginning from 13th century onwards. Linguistically modern Assamese traces its roots to the version developed by the American Missionaries based on the local form in practice near Xiwoxagor/Sibsagar district. Assamese or Oxomeeya (as called in Assam) is a rich language due to its hybrid nature with its unique characteristics of pronunciation and softness. Assamese literature is one of the richest. The constitution of India recognises it as a major language of Republic of India.

Bodo is the ancient language of Assam and is mother of majority of the present day languages and dialects within the state and also in surrounding areas. Looking at the spatial distribution patterns of related ethno-cultural groups and their cultural traits and also phenomenon such as of naming all the major rivers in the North East Region with original Bodo words (*e.g.* Dihing, Dibru, Dihong, D/Tista, Dikrai, etc.) it is understood that it was the most important language in the North East India in the ancient times, where history yet haven't opened its gates.

Bodo is presently spoken largely in the Lower Assam areas mostly under the areas of Bodo Territorial Council. During past few decades (after years of neglect) it is fortunate that Bodo as a language is getting attention and much care is being taken for development of Bodo literature.

Assam is also rich with several native languages such as Micing, Karbi, Dimaca, Rabha, Tiwa, etc. of Tibeto-Burman origin and are closely related to Bodo. There are also small groups of people in different part of Assam with languages such as Tai-Phake, Tai-Aiton, Tai-Khamti, etc. related to Tai-group of languages of Southern China and South East Asia. The Tai-Ahom language (brought by Sukaphaa and his followers) is now fortunately getting attentions for wide-spread research after centuries long care and preservation by the Bailungs (traditional priests), which is no more a spoken language for commons today. There are also small groups of people speaking Manipuri, Khasi, Garo, Hmar, Kuki, etc. in different parts of Assam.

In the past century migration of Bengalis to the medieval kingdom of Kacar (of Kocaries) in the Barak Valley has led to their majority, prompting the government of Assam to include Bengali as the official language in the Barak Valley districts.

ASSAMESE LANGUAGE

Assamese or Asamiya is an Eastern Indo-Aryan language spoken mainly in the Indian state of Assam, where it is an official language. It is the easternmost indigenous Indo-European language; it is spoken by over 15 million native speakers, and serves as a *lingua franca* in the region. It is also spoken in parts of Arunachal Pradesh and other northeast Indian states. Nagamese, an Assamese-based Creole language is widely used in Nagaland and parts of Assam. Nefamese is an Assamese-based pidgin used in Arunachal Pradesh. Small pockets of Assamese speakers can be found in Bangladesh. The non-linguistic Bengali dialects of Sylhet and northeast Bangladesh are linguistically closer to Assamese. In the past, it was the court language of the Ahom kingdom from the 17th century.

It is believed that along with other Eastern Indo-Aryan languages, Assamese evolved at least before 7th century CE from the middle Indo-Aryan Magadhi Prakrit, which developed from dialects similar to, but in some ways more archaic than Vedic Sanskrit. Its sister languages include Koch Rajbongsi, Mymensinghiya, Sylheti, Hajong (though it's a Mixed language of Sino-Tibetan origin), Bishnupriya Manipuri, Nokhailla, Chittagonian, Rohingya, Chakma, Bengali, Maithili and Angika. It is written in the Assamese script, an abugidasystem, from left to right, with a large number of typographic ligatures.

History

Assamese originated in Old Indo-Aryan dialects, though the exact nature of its origin and growth is not clear yet. It is generally believed that Assamese (Assam) and the Kamatapuri lects (Cooch Bihar and Assam) derive from the Kamarupi dialect of Eastern Magadhi Prakrit by keeping to the north of the Ganges; though some authors contest a close connection of Assamese with Magadhi Prakrit. The Indo-Aryan language in Kamarupa had differentiated by the 7th-century, before it did in Bengal or Orissa.These changes were likely due to non-Indo-Aryan speakers adopting the language. The evidence of this language (Kamarupi Prakrit) is found in the Prakritisms of the Kamarupa inscriptions. The earliest forms of Assamese in literature are found in the ninth-century Buddhist verses called Charyapada , and in 12-14th century works of Ramai Pundit (*Sunya Puran*), Boru Chandidas (*Krishna Kirtan*), Sukur Mamud (*Gopichandrar Gan*), Durllava Mullik (*Gobindachandrar Git*) and Bhavani Das (*Mainamatir Gan*). In these works, Assamese features coexist with features from other Modern Indian Languages.

A fully distinguished literary form (poetry) appeared first in the fourteenth century—in the courts of the Kamata kingdom and in the courts of an eastern Kachari king where Madhav Kandali translated the Ramayana into the Assamese (Saptakanda Ramayana). From the fifteenth and sixteenth centuries, songs – *Borgeets*, dramas – *Ankiya Naat* and the first prose writings (by Bhattadeva) were composed. The literary language, based on the western dialects of Assam moved to the court of the Ahom kingdom in the seventeenth century, where it became the state language. This period saw the widespread development of standardized prose infused with colloquial forms in Buranjis.

According to Goswami (2003), this included "the colloquial prose of religious biographies, the archaic prose of magical charms, the conventional prose of utilitarian literature on medicine, astrology, arithmetic, dance and music, and above all the standardized prose of the Buranjis. The literary language, having become infused with the eastern idiom, became the standard literary form in the nineteenth century, when the British adopted it for state purposes. As the political and commercial center shifted to Guwahati after the mid-twentieth century, the literary form moved away from the eastern variety to take its current form.

Geographical distribution

Assamese is native to Brahmaputra Valley consisting of western and eastern Assam. It is also spoken in states of Arunachal Pradeshand Nagaland. Presence of Assamese script can be found in Rakhine state of present Myanmar. Pashupati temple in Nepal also have inscription in Assamese showing its influence and prosperity in the past. There are also significant Assamese-speaking communities in Australia, Dubai, the United Kingdom, Canada, Nepal and the United States.

Official status

Assamese is the official language of Assam, and one of the 23 official languages recognised by the Republic of India. The Assam Secretariat functions in Assamese.

Phonology

The Assamese phonemic inventory consists of eight vowels, ten diphthongs, and twenty-three consonants (including two semivowels).

Consonant clusters

Consonant clusters in Assamese include thirty three pure consonant letters in the Assamese alphabet. Each letter represents a single sound with an inherent vowel, the short vowel /*a*/.

The first twenty-five consonants letters are called "sparxa barna". These "sparxa barnas" are again divided into five "bargs". Therefore, these twenty-five letters are also called "bargia barna".

Alveolar stops

The Assamese phoneme inventory is unique in the Indic group of languages in its lack of a dental-retroflex distinction among the coronal stops. Historically, the dental and retroflex series merged into alveolar stops. This makes Assamese resemble non-Indic languages of Northeast India (such as Austroasiatic and Sino-Tibetan languages). The only other language to have fronted retroflex stops into alveolars is the closely related eastern dialects of Bengali (although a contrast with dental stops remains in those dialects). Note that /r/ is normally realized as [ɹ] or as a retroflex approximant.

Voiceless velar fricative

Assamese and Sylheti are unusual among Eastern Indo-Aryan languages for the presence of the /x/ (which, phonetically, varies between velar ([x]) and a uvular ([÷]) pronunciations, depending on the speaker and speech register), historically the MIA sibilant has lenited to /x/ and /h/ (non-initially). The derivation of the velar fricative from the coronal sibilant /s/is evident in the name of the language in Assamese; some Assamese prefer to write 'Oxomiya' or 'Ôxômiya' instead of 'Asomiya' or 'Asamiya' to reflect the sound change. The voiceless velar fricative is absent in the West Goalpariya dialects though it is found in lesser extent in East Goalpariya and Kamrupi, otherwise used extensively further east. The change of /s/ to /h/ and then to /x/; all these have been attributed to Tibeto-Burman influence by Dr. Chatterjee.

Velar nasal

Assamese, Odia and Bengali, in contrast to other Indo-Aryan languages, use the velar nasal (the English *ng* in *sing*) extensively. In many languages, while the velar nasal is commonly restricted to preceding velar sounds, in Assamese it can occur intervocalically. This is another feature it shares with other languages of Northeast India, though in Assamese the velar nasal never occurs word-initially.

Writing system

Modern Assamese uses the Assamese script, and in the medieval times the script came in three varieties: *Bamuniya*,

Garhgaya and *Kaitheli* or *Lakhari*, which developed from the Kamarupi script. It very closely resembles the Mithilakshar script of the Maithili language, as well as the Bengali script. There is a strong literary tradition from early times. Examples can be seen in edicts, land grants and copper plates of medieval kings. Assam had its own system of writing on the bark of the *saanchi* tree in which religious texts and chronicles were written. The present-day spellings in Assamese are not necessarily phonetic. *Hemkosh* (হেমকোষ [ɦɛmkʊx]), the second Assamese dictionary, introduced spellings based on Sanskrit, which are now the standard.

Morphology and grammar

The Assamese language has the following characteristic morphological features:

- Gender and number are not grammatically marked.
- There is lexical distinction of gender in the third person pronoun.
- Transitive verbs are distinguished from intransitive.
- The agentive case is overtly marked as distinct from the accusative.
- Kinship nouns are inflected for personal pronominal possession.
- Adverbs can be derived from the verb roots.
- A passive construction may be employed idiomatically.

Negativization process

Verbs in Assamese are negativized by adding /n/ before the verb, with /n/ picking up the initial vowel of the verb. For example:

- /na laga/ 'do(es) not want' (1st, 2nd and 3rd persons)
- /ni lik^{h}u/ 'will not write' (1st person)
- /nukutu/ 'will not nibble' (1st person)
- /nɛlɛk^{h}ɛ/ 'does not write' (3rd person)
- /nɔkɔɹɔ/ 'do not do' (2nd person)

Dialects

Regional dialects

The language has quite a few regional variations. Banikanta Kakati identified two broad dialects which he named (1) Eastern and (2) Western dialects, of which the eastern dialect is homogeneous, and prevalent to the east of Guwahati, and the western dialect is heterogeneous. However, recent linguistic studies have identified four dialect groups listed below from east to west:

- Eastern group in and around Sivasagar District, i.e., the regions of the former undivided Sivasagar district, areas of the present day Golaghat, Jorhat and Sivasagar
- Central group in Nagaon, Sonitpur, Morigaon districts and adjoining areas
- Kamrupi group primarily in the Kamrup region, Darrang, Barpeta (Barpetia).
- Goalpariya group in the Goalpara region

Comparison

Collected from Gierson's linguistic Survey of India. The translations are not close to literal:

English: A man had two sons. The younger son told his father, 'I want my share of your estate now before you die.' So his father agreed to divide his wealth between his sons. A few days later this younger son packed all his belongings and moved to a distant land, and there he wasted all his money in wild living. About the time his money ran out, a great famine swept over the land, and he began to starve. He persuaded a local farmer to hire him, and the man sent him into his fields to feed the pigs. The young man became so hungry that even the pods he was feeding the pigs looked good to him. But no one gave him anything. When he finally came to his senses, he said to himself, 'At home even the hired servants have food enough to spare, and here I am dying of hunger!'

Eastern Assamese: Künü ezon manuhor duta putek asil; tare xorütüe bapekok köle, he deuta, xompottir zi bhag müt pore tak mük dia. Tate teü apün xompotti xibilakok bãti dile. Tar olop dinor pase xei xoru puteke xokolüke gütai dur dexoloi prosthan kori, tate lompot asoronere tar xompotti opobyoe korile. Xi xokolü byoe korilot xei dexor bor akal hól. Tate xi kosto paboloi dhorile. Tetia xi goi xei dexor ezon manuhor asroe lolot, xei manuhe tak gahori soraboloi apün potharoloi pothai dile. Tate xi gahorie khüa ebidh gosor seire pet bhoraboloi bor hepah korileü tak küneü ekü nidile. Xexot xi seton pai kóle, mür büpair koto sakore, zürakoi aru tatkoiü odhik khüa bostu paise, kintu moi iat bhükote morisü.

Central Assamese: Manhu ezono duta putak asil. Tahãtüü bhitoot xoutü putake bapekok kola,

Kamrupi: Eta manhur duta putak asil. Tahãtor bhitorot xorutü putake bapakok kolak, "Bapa! Moi zi bostur bhag pam tak mük di! Tate xi tahãtor bhitorot bostu bhag kori dilak. Olop dinor pasot xorutü putake xomuday kheni bostu log kori loi dur dexok lagi gel aro tat zai dhangkhila kori apünar bostu kheni nosto korilak. Xi tar gütai kheni bostu khoros kori phelüat pasot xei dexot eta bor dangar akal höl. Aro tar khabalobar nohüa hoba dhorilak. Tetia xi zai xer dexor ek girir log lagil. Xei manhutüi tak tar potharot bora saribak legi khedelak. Pasot borai zi xukti khai take khai tar pet bhorabak legu parileü tar bhal lagat poril. Kintu tak kaüei ekü nedlak. Xi zetia nizor opokormo buziba parilak xi tetia kolak, mür bapar kiman dormaha khaüa sakareü tahãtor laga khenitkeü besi khaüba bostu pae aro moi iat bhukhot moriba dhorisü.

Goalpariya (western) : Ek zonkar dui beta asil. Tar bhitrot söto beta tar bapok koil, "Baba, girostir ze bhag mui paim ta mök de." Tate tãe tamar mazot girosti batia dil. Olpo koe din pasot söto beta soub ekete koria durantor ek deshot paitra koril. Se desot zaea dhuddami koria aponar ghor girosti uraia dil. Tãe soub khoroc koria phelar pasot sei desot boro mongga hoil tãeö boro kostot poril. Tar pasot tãe zaea sei deser ekzon girir kasot zaea auzil. Tãe tak aponar patarot suor corbar patea dil. Pasot suore ze cokla khae, tak khaea pet bhorbar haus kolleo, kintuk kãeö tak dil na. Pasot ceton paea tãe koil, "Amar baper koto maina khaöa cakor ek pala koria khabar pae ar mui ete bhögot moribar dhorcung.

Non-regional dialects

Assamese does not have caste- or occupation-based dialects. In the nineteenth century, the Eastern dialect became the standard dialect because it witnessed more literary activity and it was more uniform from east of Guwahati to Sadiya, whereas the western dialects were more heterogeneous. Since the nineteenth century, the center of literary activity (as well as of politics and commerce) has shifted to Guwahati; as a result, the standard dialect has evolved considerably away from the largely rural Eastern dialects and has become more urban and acquired western dialectal elements. Most literary activity takes place in this dialect, and is often called the *likhito-bhaxa*, though regional dialects are often used in novels and other creative works.

In addition to the regional variants, sub-regional, community-based dialects are also prevalent, namely:

- Standard dialect influenced by surrounding centers.
- *Bhakatiya* dialect highly polite, sattra-based dialect with a different set of nominals, pronominals and verbal forms, as well as a preference for euphemism; indirect and passive expressions. Some of these features are used in the standard dialect on very formal occasions.
- The fisherman community has a dialect that is used in the central and eastern region.
- The astrologer community of Darrang district has a dialect called *thar* that is coded and secretive. The *ratikhowa* and *bhitarpanthiya* secretive cult-based Vaisnava groups too have their own dialects.
- The Muslim community have their own dialectal preference, with their own kinship, custom and religious terms, with those in east Assam having distinct phonetic features.

- The urban adolescent and youth communities (for example, Guwahati) have exotic, hybrid and local slangs.
- Ethnic speech communities that use Assamese as a second language, often use dialects that are influenced heavily by the pronunciation, intonation, stress, vocabulary and syntax of their respective first languages (*Mising Eastern Assamese, Bodo Central Kamrupi, Rabha Eastern Goalpariya* etc.). Two independent pidgins/creoles, associated with the Assamese language, are Nagamese (used by Naga groups) and Nefamese (used in Arunachal Pradesh).

Literature

There is a growing and strong body of literature in this language. The first characteristics of this language are seen in the Charyapadas composed in between the eighth and twelfth centuries.

The first examples emerged in writings of court poets in the fourteenth century, the finest example of which is Madhav Kandali's Saptakanda Ramayana. The popular ballad in the form of Ojapali is also regarded as well-crafted. The sixteenth and seventeenth centuries saw a flourishing of Vaishnavite literature, leading up to the emergence of modern forms of literature in the late nineteenth century.

ASSAMESE LITERATURE

Assamese literature is the entire corpus of poetry, novels, short stories, documents and other writings in the Assamese language. It also includes popular ballads in the older forms of the language during its evolution to the contemporary form. The literary heritage of the Assamese language can be traced back to the c. 9-10th century in the *Charyapada*, where the earliest elements of the language can be discerned.

History

The history of the Assamese literature may be broadly divided into three periods:

Early Assamese (6th to 15th century)

Even though systematic errors in the Sanskrit of Kamarupa inscriptions betray an underlying Pakrit in the pre-12th century period,scarce examples of the language exist. The *Charyapadas*, the Buddhist ballads of 8th-10th century some of whose composers were from Kamarupa and the language of which bear strong affitinities with Assamese (beside Bengali, Maithili and Oriya), are considered the first examples of Assamese literature. The spirit of the *Charyapadas* are found in later-day *Deh-Bicaror Geet* and other aphorisms; and some of the ragas found their way to the 15th-16th century *Borgeets*. In the 12th-14th century period the works of Ramai Pundit (*Sunya Puran*), Boru Chandidas (*Krishna Kirtan*), Sukur Mamud (*Gopichandrar Gan*), Durllava Mullik (*Gobindachandrar Git*) and Bhavani Das (*Mainamatir Gan*) bear strong grammatical relationship to Assamese; and their expressions and their use of *adi-rasa* are found in the later Panchali works of Mankar and Pitambar. These works too are claimed as examples of Bengali literature. After this period of shared legacy a fully differentiated Assamese literature finally emerged in the 14th century.

Pre-Sankardeva period

This period saw the flourishing of two kinds of literary activity: translations and adaptations, and choral songs.

Translations and Adaptations

Harivara Vipra, a court poet of Durlabhnarayana (1330–1350) of Kamata, with his work *Vavruvahanar Yuddha* (based on the Mahabharata) and *Lava-Kuxar Yuddha* (based on the Ramayana) provides the first date-able examples of Assamese literature. Though translated works, they contain local descriptions and embellishments, a feature that describes all translated work of this period. His Vavruvahanar Yuddha, for instance makes references to articles of the Ahom kingdom, which at that time was a small kingdom in the east, and describes the undivided Lakhimpur region, and in *Lava-Kushar*

Yuddha he departs from the original and describes local customs for Rama and Sita's *pumsavana* ceremony. Other works in this class and period are Hema Saraswati's *Prahlada-caritra* and *Hara-Gauri-Samvada*; Kaviratna Saravati's *Jayadratha-vadha*; Rudra Kandali's *Satyaki-pravesa*. All these works are associated with Durlabhanarayan of Kamata and his immediate successors.

The major work from this period that left a lasting impression is *Saptakanda Ramayana*, composed by Madhava Kandali, and recited in the court of a 14th-century Barahi-Kachari king Mahamanikya (Mahamanikpha) who ruled either in the Nagaon or the Golaghat region. In chronology, among vernacular translations of the original Sanskrit, Kandali's Ramayana comes after Kamban's (Tamil), and ahead of Kirttivas' (Bengali, 15th century), Tulsidas' (Awadhi, 16th century), Balaram Das' (Oriya) etc. The literary language (as opposed to the colloquial Assamese) this work adopted became the standard literary language for much of the following periods, till the rise of new literature in the 19th century. That his work was a major influence can be inferred from Sankardeva's tribute to the "unerring predecessor poet". The *pada* form of metrical verse (14 syllables in each verse with identical two syllables at the end of each foot in a couplet) became a standard in Assamese *kavya* works, something that continued till the modern times. Though a translated work, it is infused with local color, and instead of the heroic, Kandali instead emphasized the homely issues of relationships etc. Among the two kinds of *alamkara's*, *arthalankaras* were used extensively, with similes and metaphors taken from the local milieu even though the original works are set in foreign lands; whereas the *shabdalankara* (alliteration etc.) were rarely used.

Choral songs

Choral songs composed for a popular form of narration-performances called *Oja-pali*, a precursor to theater and theatrical performances, came to be known as *Panchali* works. Though some of these works are contemporaneous to Sankardeva's, they hark back to older forms free of Sankardeva's influences and so are considered pre-Sankardeva literature. The *Oja-palis* follow two different traditions: *biyah-gowa* which tells stories from the Mahabharata and *Maroi*, which tells stories on the snake goddess *Manaxa*. The poets—Pitambar, Durgabar, Mankar and Sukavi Narayan—are well known for the compositions.

Middle Assamese (17th to 19th century)

This is a period of the prose chronicles (*Buranji*) of the Ahom court. The Ahoms had brought with them an instinct for historical writings. In the Ahom court, historical chronicles were at first composed in their original Tibetan-Chinese language, but when the Ahom rulers adopted Assamese as the court language, historical chronicles began to be written in Assamese. From the beginning of the 17th century onwards, court chronicles were written in large numbers. These chronicles or buranjis, as they were called by the Ahoms, broke away from the style of the religious writers. The language is essentially modern except for slight alterations in grammar and spelling.

Modern Assamese

Effect of British rule

The British imposed Bengali in 1836 in Assam after the state was occupied in 1826. Due to a sustained campaign, Assamese was reinstated in 1873 as the state language. Since the initial printing and literary activity occurred in eastern Assam, the Eastern dialect was introduced in schools, courts and offices and soon came to be formally recognized as the Standard Assamese. In recent times, with the growth of Guwahati as the political and commercial center of Assam, the Standard Assamese has moved away from its roots in the Eastern dialect.

Influence of Missionaries

The modern Assamese period began with the publication of the Bible in Assamese prose by the American Baptistmissionaries in 1819. The currently prevalent standard Asamiya has its roots in the Sibsagar dialect of Eastern Assam. As mentioned in Bani

Kanta Kakati's "Assamese, its Formation and Development" (1941, Published by Sree Khagendra Narayan Dutta Baruah, LBS Publications, G.N. Bordoloi Road, Gauhati-1, Assam, India) – " The Missionaries made Sibsagar in Eastern Assam the centre of their activities and used the dialect of Sibsagar for their literary purposes". The American Baptist Missionaries were the first to use this dialect in translating the Bible in 1813.

The Missionaries established the first printing press in Sibsagar in 1836 and started using the local Asamiya dialect for writing purposes. In 1846 they started a monthly periodical called *Arunodoi*, and in 1848, Nathan Brown published the first book on Assamese grammar. The Missionaries published the first Assamese-English Dictionary compiled by M. Bronson in 1867. One of the major contributions of the American Baptist missionaries to the Assamese language is the reintroduction of Assamese as the official language in Assam. In 1848 missionary Nathan Brown published a treatise on the Assamese language. This treatise gave a strong impetus towards reintroducing Assamese the official language in Assam. In his 1853 official report on the province of Assam, British official Moffat Mills wrote:

"...the people complain, and in my opinion with much reason, of the substitution of Bengalee for the Vernacular Assamese. Bengalee is the language of the court, not of their popular books and shashtras, and there is a strong prejudice to its general use. ...Assamese is described by Mr. Brown, the best scholar in the province, as a beautiful, simple language, differing in more respects from, than agreeing with, Bengalee, and I think we made a great mistake in directing that all business should be transacted in Bengalee, and that the Assamese must acquire it. It is too late now to retrace our steps, but I would strongly recommend Anandaram Phukan's proposition to the favourable consideration of the Council of Education, viz., the substitution of the vernacular language in lieu of Bengalee, and completion of the course of the Vernacular education in Bengalee. I feel persuaded that a youth will, under this system of tuition, learn more in two than he now acquires in four years.

An English youth is not taught in Latin until he is well grounded in English, and in the same manner, an Assamese should not be taught in a foreign language until he knows his own."

Beginning of Modern Literature

The period of modern literature began with the publication the Assamese journal *Jonaki* (1889), which introduced the short story form first by Lakshminath Bezbaroa. Thus began the Jonaki period of Assamese literature. In 1894 Rajanikanta Bordoloi published the first Assamese novel *Mirijiyori*.

The modern Assamese literature has been enriched by the works of Jyoti Prasad Agarwalla, Birinchi Kumar Barua, Hem Barua, Atul Chandra Hazarika, Nalini Bala Devi, Navakanta Barua, Mamoni Raisom Goswami, Bhabendra Nath Saikia, Homen Borgohain, Nirupama Borgohain, Kanchan Baruah, Saurabh Kumar Chaliha and others. Moreover, as regards the spreading of Assamese literature outside Assam, the complete work of Jyoti Prasad Agarwala has been translated into Hindi to reach a wider audience by Devi Prasad Bagrodia. Bagrodia has also translated Shrimanta Shankardev's 'Gunamala' into Hindi.

In 1917 the Asam Sahitya Sabha was formed as a guardian of the Assamese society and the forum for the development of Assamese language and literature. Padmanath Gohain Baruah was the first president of the society.

Contemporary literature

Contemporary writers include Arupa Patangia Kalita,Monikuntala Bhattacharya,Mousumi Kondoli, Monalisa Saikia.

5

Geography and Flora & Fauna

GEOGRAPHY

Assam, the land of hills and valleys, the land of the mighty river Brahmaputra, the land of Mother Goddess Kamakhya, lies in the northeastern corner of India. In these pages, you will find a few glimpses of Assam and Assamese people. Assam is a land of about 25 million people situated in the northeast corner of India. The principal language of Assam is Assamese although a large number of other languages are spoken. Assam comprises an area of 78,523 square kilometers (30,318 square miles). Except for a narrow corridor running through the foothills of the Himalayas that connects the state with West Bengal, Assam is almost entirely isolated from India. The capital of Assam, is Dispur, a suburb of Guwahati in 1972.

The name "Assam" is derived from the term "Asom" which, in Sanskrit, refers to unequal or unrivalled. The uneven topography of the land, full of hills, plains and rivers might, therefore, have contributed to her name. The Mongolian Ahom dynasty which had ruled Assam for more than six hundred years might also be the cause for her name.

Assam is a land with an illustrious recorded history going back to the 4th century BC. Assam was an independent kingdom throughout all of history till the end of the first quarter of the 19th century when the British conquered the kingdom and annexed it to British India. The current state capital of Assam, Guwahati, known in ancient time as Pragjyotishpura or The Eastern City of Light, was the capital of Kamrup which finds frequent mention in the Great Hindu Epic Mahabharata and other Sanskrit volumes and historical lores.

Assam's economy is based on agriculture and oil. Assam produces a significant part of the total tea production of the world. Assam produces more than half of India's petroleum.

The current political situation in Assam is unstable with United Liberation of Asom (ULFA) fighting a low-intensity but wide-spread guerrilla warfare for independence from India. Although the Indian military has tried to quell the insurgents with a large presence for more than ten years, they have been not very successful. There are other militant groups who are seeking independence or autonomy in Assam. There have been consistent reports of grave human rights violations in Assam committed primarily by the Indian military.

The state lies beneath the foothills of the Eastern Himalayas and is bounded on the north by Bhutan (the land of the Bhutiyas) and Arunachal Pradesh (formerly known as NEFA and the land of Adis, Dafflas, Miris, Mishimis and Appatanis---all hill tribes of mongolian origin); to the east by Arunachal Pradesh, Nagaland, and Manipur (an ancient Hindu kingdom); to the south by Mizoram (the land of Mizos) and Meghalaya (the land of Khasis with Shillong, "the Scotland of east" as her capital); and to the west by Bangladesh and Tripura (the native land of the Tripuri tribes of Mongolian origin). Except for a narrow corridor running through the foothills of the Himalayas that connects the state with West Bengal, Assam is almost entirely isolated from India. The capital of Assam, is Dispur, a suburb of Guwahati in 1972.

Surrounded by a ring of blue hills, Assam has two largest valleys, the Brahmaputra Valley and the Barak Valley where the main body of the people of Assam live, the people with history dating back to ancient vedic era.

In ancient days, Assam was known as Kamrup where according to legend, Kamdeva, the Hindu God of love was reborn. The state capital of Assam, Guwahati, known in ancient time as Pragjyotishpura or The Eastern City of Light, was the capital of Kamrup which finds frequent mention in the Mahabharata and other Sanskrit epics and historical lores.

Assam comprises an area of 78,523 square kilometers (30,318 square miles). Except for the districts of Karbi Anglong and North Cachar Hills, Assam is generally composed of plains and river valleys. It can be divided into three principal geographical regions: the Brahmaputra Valley in the north; the Barak Plain in the south; and the Mikir and Cachar Hills that divide the two regions.

The Brahmaputra Valley is the dominant physical feature of Assam. It enters Assam near Sadiya at the extreme northeast corner and runs westward for nearly 450 miles before turning south to enter the plains of Bangladesh. The river valley, rarely more than 50 miles wide, is studded with numerous low, isolated hills and ridges that abruptly rise from the plain. The vally is surrounded on all sides, except the west, by mountains and is intersected by many streams and rivulets that flow from the neighbouring hills to empty into the Brahmaputra.

Earthquakes are a common phenomenon in Assam. In modern times, the most important Assamese earthquakes have been those that occurred in 1897 with the Shillong Plateau as the epicentre; in 1930 with Dhubri as the epicentre; and 1950, with Rima in Tibet at the Arunachal border as the epicentre. The 1950 earthquake is considered to have been one of the most disastrous earthquakes in history. It created heavy landslides that blocked the course of many hill streams.

The average temperature is moderate, about 84°F (29°C) in the hottest month of August. The average valley temperature in January is 61°F (16°C). In this season, the climate of the valley is marked by heavy fogs and a little rain. Assam does not have the normal Indian hot, dry season. Some rain occurs from March onwards, but the real force of the monsoon winds is faced from June onward. Rainfall in Assam ranks among the highest in the world; its annual rainfall varies from 70 inches in the west to 120 inches per year in the east. Large concentrated during the months from June to September, it often results in widespread destructive floods.

Assam's forests cover about 20 percent of the total area. The Kaziranga National Park, the stronghold of the fast-disappearing great Indian one-horned rhinoceros, is its most famous wildlife refuge. The most important forest products are timber and bamboo, firewood and lac (the source of shellac). There are about 74 species of timber, of which two-thirds are commercially exploited. The forests are inhabited by wild animals such as elephants, tigers, deer and wild pigs.

Physical Geography of Assam is extremely interesting with its geologic origin, geomorphic characteristics, climate, rich biodiversity, etc. Assam, extending from 89 degree 42 minutes E longitude to 96 degree E longitude and 24 degree 8 minutes N latitudes to 28 degree 2 minutes N latitudes in the graticule is a North Eastern state of India. Assam is located at the central part of the North-East India and with an area of 78,438 sq.km it is almost equivalent to the size of Ireland or Austria.

Assam is a north eastern state of India with its capital at Dispur, a part of Guwahati. Located south of the eastern Himalayas, Assam comprises the Brahmaputra and the Barak river valleys and the Karbi Anglong and the North Cachar Hills. With an area of 78,438 sq.km Assam currently is almost equivalent to the size of Ireland or Austria. Assam is surrounded by the rest of the *Seven Sister States*: Arunachal Pradesh, Nagaland, Manipur, Mizoram, Tripura and Meghalaya.

These states are connected to the rest of India via a narrow strip in West Bengal called the "Chicken's Neck." Assam also shares international borders with Bhutan and Bangladesh; and cultures, peoples and climate with South-East Asia—important elements in India's Look East Policy.

Assam is known for Assam tea, petroleum resources, Assam silk and for its rich biodiversity. It has successfully conserved the one-horned Indian rhinoceros from near extinction in Kaziranga, the tiger in Manas and provides one of the last wild habitats for the Asian elephant. It is increasingly becoming a popular destination for wild-life tourism and notably Kaziranga and Manas are both World Heritage Sites. Assam was also known for its Sal tree forests and forest products, much depleted now. A land of high rainfall, Assam is endowed with lush greenery and the mighty river Brahmaputra, its tributaries and oxbow lakes provide the region with a unique hydro-geomorphic and aesthetic environment.

PHYSICAL GEOGRAPHY OF ASSAM

This article discusses the geological origin, geomorphic characteristics, and climate of the northeastern Indian state of Assam. Extending from 89° 422 E to 96° E longitude and 24° 82 N to 28° 22 N latitude, it has an area of 78,438 km, similar to that of Ireland or Austria.

Geologic and geomorphic origin

Geologically, as per the plate tectonics, Assam is in the eastern most projection of the Indian Plate, where it thrusts underneath the Eurasian Plate creating a subduction zone. It is postulated that due to the northeasterly movement of the Indian plate, the sedimentary layers of an ancient geocyncline called the Tethys (in between Indian and Eurasian Plates) were pushed upward to form the Himalayas. It is estimated that the height of the Himalayas is increasing by 4 cm each year. Therefore, Assam possesses a special geomorphic environment, with large plains and dissected hills of the South Indian Plateau system abutting the Himalayas to the north, north-east and east.

Geomorphic studies also conclude that the Brahmaputra is an antecedent river, older than the Himalayas, which often crosses higher altitudes in the Himalayas eroding at a greater pace than the increase in the height of the mountain range to sustain its flow. The height of the surrounding regions still increasing forming steep gorges in Arunachal.

Physiography

Entering Assam, the Brahmaputra becomes a braided river, and, along with its tributaries, creates the flood plain of the Brahmaputra Valley. The Brahmaputra Valley in Assam is approximately 80 to 100 km wide and almost 1000 km long. The width of the river itself is 16 km at many places within the valley.

The hills of Karbi Anglong and Dima Hasao district and those in and around Guwahati and North Guwahati (along with the Khasi and Garo Hills) are originally parts of the South Indian Plateau system. These are eroded and dissected by the numerous rivers in the region. Average height of these hills in Assam varies from 300 to 400m.

The southern Barak Valley is separated by the Karbi Anglong and North Cachar Hills from the Brahmaputra Valley in Assam. The Barak originates from the Barail Range in the border areas of Assam, Nagaland and Manipur and flowing through the district of Cachar, it confluences with the Brahmaputra in Bangladesh. Barak Valley in Assam is a small valley with an average width and length of approximately 40 to 50 km.

Mineral resources

Assam is endowed with petroleum, natural gas, coal, limestone and many other minor minerals such as magnetic quartzite, kaolin, sillimanites, clay and feldspar. A small quantity of iron ore is also available in western parts of Assam.

The Upper Assam districts are major reserves of oil and gas. Petroleum was discovered in Assam in 1889. It is estimated that Assam and surrounding region possess around 150 million tonnes of petroleum reserves. Presently, Assam is the 3rd largest producer of petroleum (crude) and natural gas in the country accounting for 16% and 8% respectively of the total production of this mineral in the country.

A Tertiary coal belt is located in Tinsukia, Dibrugarh, Sivasagar, Karbi Anglong and Dima Hasao districts with an estimated reserve of 370 million tonnes. Assam coal is friable in nature and has a high sulphur content. It is mainly utilised by local railways, steamers, and hydro power stations. Low moisture, low volatile cooking coal has been discovered in the Hallidayganj Singrimari area.

Assam has rich limestone reserves. The major reserves of limestone are in Dima Hasao and Karbi Anglong districts. A total reserve of 97 million tonnes of limestone has been found in these two districts and almost half of the reserve is of cement grade. Moreover, there is an estimated reserve of 365 million tonnes of limestone near Umrangshu in Dima Hasao district. Among the minor minerals, there are quartzite reserves in the Nagaon district, kaolin reserves in Karbi Anglong and the Lakhimpur districts and sillimanite-bearing rocks in Karbi Anglong district.

Climatic characteristics

With the 'Tropical Monsoon Rainforest Climate', Assam is a temperate region and experiences heavy rainfall and humidity. Winter lasts from late October to late February. The minimum temperature is 6 to 8 degrees Celsius. Nights and early mornings are foggy, and rain is scanty. Summer starts in mid May, accompanied by high humidity and rainfall. The maximum temperature is 35 to 38 degrees Celsius, but the frequent rain reduces this. The peak of the monsoons is during June. Thunderstorms known as *Bordoicila* are frequent during the afternoons.

Biogeography and biodiversity

There are a number of tropical rainforests in Assam, including the Dehing Patkai rainforest. Moreover, there are riverine grass lands, bambooorchards and numerous wetland ecosystems. Many of these areas have been protected by developing national parks and reserved forests. The Kaziranga and Manas are the two World Heritage Sites in the region. The Kaziranga is the home for the rare Indian rhinoceros, while Manas is a tiger sanctuary.

Apart from the rhinoceros and the tiger, the spotted deer or chital / *futukihorina* (*Axis axis*), the swamp deer or *dolharina* (*Cervus duvauceli duvauceli*), the clouded leopard (*Neofelis nebulosa*), the hoolock gibbon or *holoubandor*, pygmy hog or *nol-gahori* (*Sus salvanis*), the wild buffalo, the hispid hare, the golden langur (*Chloropsis cochinchinensis*), the golden cat, the giant civet, the binturong, the hog badger, the civet cat and the porcupine are all found in the state. Moreover, there are abundant numbers of Gangetic dolphins, mongooses, giant squirrels and pythons.

A few of the major birds in Assam are: the blue-throated barbet or *hetuluka* (*Megalaima asiatica*), the white-winged wood duck or *deuhnah*(*Cairina scultulata*), the Pallas's fish eagle or *kuruwa* (*Haliaeetus leucoryphus*), the great pied hornbill or *rajdhonesh* (*Buceros bicornis homrai*), the Himalayan golden-backed three-toed woodpecker or *barhoituka* (*Dinopium shorii shorii*), and the migratory pelican.

Assam is also known for orchids and also for valuable plant species and forest products.

Natural disasters

The region is also prone to natural disasters. High rainfall, deforestation, and other factors which have resulted in annual floods. These often cause widespread loss of life, livelihood and property. The region is also prone to earthquake, mild tremors are common, but strong earthquakes are rare. There have been three strong earthquakes: in 1869 the bank of the Barak sank by 15 ft. In 1897 there was a tremor which measured 8.3 on the moment magnitude scale, and another in 1950 which measured 8.6.

BIODIVERSITY OF ASSAM

The biodiversity of Assam, a state in North-East India, makes it a biological hotspot with many rare and endemic plant and animal species. The greatest success in recent years has been the conservation of the Indian rhinoceros at the Kaziranga National Park, but a rapid increase in human population in

Assam threatens many plants and animals and their natural habitats.

The rhinoceros, tiger, deer or chital / *futukihorina* (*Axis axis*), swamp deer or *dolhorina* (*Cervus duvauceli duvauceli*), clouded leopard(*Neofelis nebulosa*), hoolock gibbon, pygmy hog or *nol-gahori* (*Porcula salvania*), hispid hare, golden langur (*Trachypithecus geei*), golden cat, giant civet, binturong, hog badger, porcupine, and civet are found in Assam. Moreover, there are abundant numbers of Gangetic dolphins, mongooses, giant squirrels and pythons. The largest population of wild water buffalo anywhere is in Assam.

The major birds in Assam include the blue-throated barbet or *hetuluka* (*Megalaima asiatica*), white-winged wood duck or *deuhnah*(*Asarcornis scultulata*), ring-tailed fishing eagle or *kuruwa* (*Haliaeetus leucorythus*), great pied hornbill or *rajdhonesh* (*Buceros bicornis homrai*), Himalayan golden-backed three-toed wood-pecker or *barhoituka* (*Dinopium shorii shorii*), and migratory pelican.

Assam is also known for orchids and for valuable plant species and forest products.

6

Economy

INTRODUCTION

Assam's economy is based on agriculture and oil. Assam produces more than half of India's tea. The Assam-Arakan basin holds about a quarter of the country's oil reserves, and produces about 12% of its total petroleum. According to the recent estimates, Assam's per capita GDP is 6,157 at constant prices (1993–94) and 10,198 at current prices; almost 40% lower than that in India. According to the recent estimates, per capita income in Assam has reached 6756 (1993–94 constant prices) in 2004–05, which is still much lower than India's.

Macro-economy

The economy of Assam today represents a unique juxtaposition of backwardness amidst plenty. Despite its rich natural resources, and supplying of up to 25% of India's petroleum needs, Assam's growth rate has not kept pace with that of India; the difference has increased rapidly since the 1970s.

The Indian economy grew at 6% per annum over the period of 1981 to 2000; the growth rate of Assam was only 3.3%. In the Sixth Plan period, Assam experienced a negative growth rate of 3.78% when India's was positive at 6%. In the post-liberalised era (after 1991), the difference widened further.

According to recent analysis, Assam's economy is showing signs of improvement. In 2001–02, the economy grew (at 1993–94 constant prices) at 4.5%, falling to 3.4% in the next financial year. During 2003–04 and 2004–05, the economy grew (at 1993–94 constant prices) at 5.5% and 5.3% respectively. The advanced estimates placed the growth rate for 2005–06 at above 6%. Assam's GDP in 2004 is estimated at $13 billion in current prices. Sectoral analysis again exhibits a dismal picture. The average annual growth rate of agriculture, which was 2.6% per annum over the 1980s, has fallen to 1.6% in the 1990s. The manufacturing sector showed some improvement in the 1990s with a growth rate of 3.4% per annum than 2.4% in the 1980s. For the past five decades, the tertiary sector has registered the highest growth rates of the other sectors, which even has slowed down in the 1990s than in the 1980s.

Economy of Assam

The Economy of Assam is largely agriculture based with 69% of the population engaged in it. Principal Bhabananda Deka was the first Assamese Economist and Research Scholar to initiate formal extensive research on economy of Assam for five centuries right from the time of Srimanta Sankardev. His research based book *Asomor Arthaneeti*(Economy of Assam) is acknowledged as the first ever research based Assamese book on Assam Economics.

The first edition of this historic milestone book was published in 1963. Over the years, he authored 115(one hundred fifteen) books encompassing economics, heritage, tribal studies and ancient literature of Assam. All the present scholars, teachers and students of economics in Assam read and refer to his books on economics, and follow in the path shown by him till his day of death on 4 December 2006. A documentary film *Golden Jubilee of Assam Economics Research & Pioneer Assam Economist-Litterateur* was officially released in 2014 commemorating completion of 50 years of publication of first Assamese book on economy of Assam by the pioneer Assam economist Principal Bhabananda Deka.

Macro-economic trend

Economy of Assam today represents a unique juxtaposition of backwardness amidst plenty. Growth rate of Assam's income has not kept pace with that of India's during the Post-British Era; differences increased rapidly since the 1970s.While the Indian economy grew at 6 percent per annum over the period of 1981 to 2000, the same of Assam's grew only by 3.3 percent.

In the Sixth Plan period Assam experienced a negative growth rate of 3.78 percent against a growth rate of 6 percent of India's. In the post-liberalised era (after 1991), the gaps between growth rates of Assam's and India's economy widened further.

In the current decade, according to recent analysis, Assam's economy is showing signs of improvement.

In the year 2001-2002, the economy grew in 1993-94 constant prices at 4.5 percent, falling to 3.4 percent in the next financial year. During 2003-2004 and 2004-2005, in the same constant prices, the economy grew more satisfactorily at 5.5 and 5.3 percent respectively.

The advanced estimates placed the growth rate for the year 2005-2006 at above 6 percent.

In the 1950s, soon after the independence, per capita income in Assam was little higher than that in India; it is much lower today.

In the year 2000-2001, per capita income in Assam was INR 6,157 at constant prices (1993–94) and INR 10,198 at current prices, which is almost 40 percent lower than that in India. According to the recent estimates, per capita income in Assam at 1993-94 constant prices has reached INR 6520 in 2003-2004 and INR 6756 in 2004-2005, which is still much lower than the same of India.

This is a chart of trend of gross state domestic product of Assam at market prices estimated by *Ministry of Statistics and Programme Implementation* with figures in millions of Indian Rupees.

Year	Gross State Domestic Product
1980	25,160
1985	56,730
1990	106,210
1995	194,110
2000	314,760

Assam's gross state domestic product for 2004 is estimated at $13 billion in current prices.

Sectoral analysis again exhibits a dismal picture. The average annual growth rate of agriculture, which was only 2.6 percent per annum over 1980s fellto 1.6 percent in the 1990s.The manufacturing sector showed some improvement in the 1990s with a growth rate of 3.4 percent per annum than 2.4 percent in the 1980s. In the past five decades, the tertiary sector has registered the highest growth rates than the primary and secondary sectors, which even has slowed down in the 1990s than in the 1980s.

Agriculture and Livestock

Agriculture accounts for more than a third of Assam's income and employs 69 percent of total workforce. Assam's biggest contribution to the world is its tea. Assam produces some of the finest and most expensive teas in the world. Other than the Chinese tea variety *Camellia sinensis*, Assam is the only region in the world that has its own variety of tea, called *Camellia assamica.*

Assam tea is grown at elevations near sea level, giving it a malty sweetness and an earthy flavor, as opposed to the more floral aroma of highland (e.g. Darjeeling, Taiwanese) teas. Assam also accounts for fair share of India's production of rice, rapeseed, mustard, jute, potato, sweet potato, banana, papaya, areca nut and turmeric. Assam is also a home of large varieties of citrus fruits, leaf vegetables, vegetables, useful grasses, herbs, spices, etc. which are mostly subsistence crops.

A tea garden in Assam

Given below is a table of 2015 national output share of select agricultural crops and allied segments in Assam based on 2011 prices

Segment	National Share %
Tea	60.0
Pineapple	18.1
Arecanut	14.8
Narcotics	12.7
Jackfruit	10.4
Garlic	9.8
Ginger	9.3
Cabbage	9.1
Inland fish	9.0
Radish	8.5
Cucumber	7.4

Orange	7.0
Niger seed	6.5
Litchi	6.1
Carrot	6.0
Jute	5.9
Condiments and spices	5.6
Coffee	5.3
Betel	5.1
Bitter gourd	5.1

Assam's agriculture has yet to experience modernisation in a real sense and is lagging behind. With implications to food security, per capita food grain production has declined in past five decades. On the other hand, although productivity of crops increased marginally, still these are much lower in comparison to highly productive regions. For instance, yield of rice, which is staple food of Assam, was just 1531 kg per hectare against India's 1927 kg per hectare in 2000-2001 (which itself is much lower than Egypt's 9283, United States's 7279, South Korea's 6838, Japan's 6635 and China's 6131 kg per hectare in 2001). On the other hand, although having a strong domestic demand, 1.5 million hectares of inland water bodies and numerous rivers and streams and 165 varieties of fishes, fishing is still in its traditional form and production is not self-sufficient.

Oil and Gas

Assam is a major producer of crude oil and natural gas in India. It was the second place in the world (after Titusville in the United States) where petroleum was discovered. Asia's first successful mechanically drilled oil well was drilled in Makum (Assam) way back in 1867. The second oldest oil well in the world still produces crude oil. Most of the oilfields of Assam are located in the Upper Assam region of the Brahmaputra Valley. Assam has four oil refineries located at Guwahati, Digboi, Numaligarh and Bongaigaon with a total capacity of 7 MMTPA (Million Metric Tonnes per annum). Bongaigaon Refinery and Petrochemicals Limited (BRPL) is the only *S&P CNX 500* conglomerate with corporate office in Assam.One of the biggest public sector oil company of the country, Oil India Ltd. has its plant and headquarter at Duliajan.

Other Industries

Apart from tea and petroleum refineries, Assam has few industries of significance. Industrial development is inhibited by its physical and political isolation from neighbouring countries such as Myanmar, China and Bangladesh and from the other growing South East Asian economies. The region is landlocked and situated in the eastern most periphery of India and is linked to the mainland of India by a flood and cyclone prone narrow corridor with weak transportation infrastructure. The international airport in Guwahati is yet to find airlines providing better direct international flights. The Brahmaputra suitable for navigation does not have sufficient infrastructure for international trade and success of such a navigable trade route will be dependent on proper channel maintenance, and diplomatic and trade relationships with Bangladesh.

Although having a poor overall industrial performance, there are several other industries, including a chemical fertiliser plant at Namrup, petrochemical industries at Namrup and Bongaigaon, paper mills at Jagiroad, Panchgram and Jogighopa, sugar mills at Barua Bamun Gaon, Chargola, Kampur, cement plant at Bokajan, cosmetics plant of Hindustan Unilever(HUL) at Doom Dooma, etc. Moreover, there are other industries such as jute mill, textile and yarn mills, silk mill, etc. Many of these industries are facing loss and closer due to lack of infrastructure and improper management practices.

EMPLOYMENT

Unemployment is one of the major problems of Assam which can be attributed to overpopulation, and a faulty education system. Every year, large numbers of students obtain higher academic degrees but because of non-availability of proportional vacancies, most of these students remain unemployed. A number of employers hire over-qualified or efficient, but under-certified, candidates, or candidates with narrowly defined qualifications. The problem is exacerbated by the growth in the number of technical institutes in Assam which increases the unemployed community of the State. Many job-seekers are eligible for jobs in sectors like Railways and Oil India but don't get these jobs because of the appointment of candidates from outside of Assam to these posts. The reluctance on the part of the departments concerned to advertise vacancies in vernacular language has also made matters worse for local unemployed youths particularly for the job-seekers of Grade C and D vacancies.

Reduction of the unemployed has been threatened by illegal immigration from Bangladesh. This has increased the workforce without a commensurate increase in jobs. Immigrants compete with local workers for jobs at lower wages, particularly in construction, domestics, Rickshaw-pullers, and vegetable sellers. The government has been identifying (via NRC) and deporting illegal immigrants. Continued immigration is exceeding deportation.

Agriculture

In Assam among all the productive sectors, agriculture makes the highest contribution to its domestic sectors, accounting for more than a third of Assam's income and employs 69% of workforce. Assam's biggest contribution to the world is Assam tea. It has its own variety, *Camellia sinensis* var. *assamica*. The state produces rice, rapeseed, mustard seed, jute, potato, sweet potato, banana, papaya, areca nut, sugarcane and turmeric.

Assam's agriculture is yet to experience modernisation in a real sense. With implications for food security, per capita food grain production has declined in the past five decades. Productivity has increased marginally, but is still low compared to highly productive regions. For instance, the yield of rice (staple food of Assam) was just 1531 kg per hectare against India's 1927 kg per hectare in 2000–01 (which itself is much lower than Egypt's 9283, US's 7279, South Korea's 6838, Japan's 6635 and China's 6131 kg per hectare in 2001). On the other hand, after having strong domestic demand, and with 1.5 million hectares of inland water bodies, numerous rivers and 165 varieties of fishes, fishing is still in its traditional form and production is not self-sufficient.

Flood in Assam greatly affects the farmers and the families dependent on agriculture because of large-scale damage of agricultural fields and crops by flood water. Every year, flooding from the Brahmaputra and other rivers deluges places in Assam. The water levels of the rivers rise because of rainfall resulting in the rivers overflowing their banks and engulfing nearby areas. Apart from houses and livestock being washed away by flood water, bridges, railway tracks and roads are also damaged by the calamity, which causes communication breakdown in many places. Fatalities are also caused by the natural disaster in many places of the State.

Industry

Assam's proximity to some neighbouring countries such as Bangladesh, Nepal and Bhutan, benefits its trade. The major Border checkpoints through which border trade flows to Bangladesh from Assam are :- Sutarkandi (Karimganj), Dhubri, Mankachar (Dhubri) and Golokanj. To facilitate border trade with Bangladesh, Border Trade Centres have been developed at Sutarkandi and Mankachar. It has been proposed in the 11th five-year plan to set up two more Border Trade Center, one at Ledo connecting China and other at Darrang connecting Bhutan. There are several Land Custom Stations (LCS) in the state bordering Bangladesh and Bhutan to facilitate border trade.

The government of India has identified some thrust areas for industrial development of Assam:

- Petroleum and natural gas-based industries
- Industries based on locally available minerals
- Processing of plantation crops
- Food processing industries
- Agri-Horticulture products

- Agri-Horticulture products
- Herbal products
- Biotech products
- Pharmaceuticals
- Chemical and plastic-based industries
- Export oriented industries
- Electronic and IT base industries including services sector
- Paper making industries
- Textiles and sericulture
- Engineering industries
- Cane and bamboo-based industries
- Other handicrafts industry

Although, the region in the eastern periphery of India is landlocked and is linked to the mainland by the narrow Siliguri Corridor (or the Chicken's Neck) improved transport infrastructure in all the three modes — rail, road and air — and developing urban infrastructure in the cities and towns of Assam are giving a boost to the entire industrial scene. The Lokpriya Gopinath Bordoloi International Airport at Guwahati, although is yet to be fully functional with international flights, was the 12th busiest airport of India in 2012. The cities of Guwahati in the West and Dibrugarh in the East with good rail, road and air connectivity are the two important nerve centres of Assam, to be selected by Asian Development Bank for providing $200 million for improvement of urban infrastructure.

Assam is a producer of crude oil and it accounts for about 15% of India's crude output, exploited by the Assam Oil Company Ltd., and natural gas in India and is the second place in the world (after Titusville in the United States) where petroleum was discovered. Asia's first successful mechanically drilled oil well was drilled in Makum way back in 1867. Most of the oilfields are located in the Eastern Assam region. Assam has four oil refineries in Digboi (Asia's first and world's second refinery), Guwahati, Bongaigaon and Numaligarhand with a total capacity of 7 million metric tonnes (7.7 million short tons) per annum. Asia's first refinery was set up at Digboi and discoverer of Digboi oilfield was the Assam Railways & Trading Company Limited (AR&T Co. Ltd.), a registered company of London in 1881. One of the biggest public sector oil company of the country Oil India Ltd. has its plant and headquarters at Duliajan.

There are several other industries, including a chemical fertiliser plant at Namrup, petrochemical industries at Namrup and Bongaigaon, Paper mills at Jagiroad, Hindustan Paper Corporation Ltd. Township Area Panchgram and Jogighopa, sugar mills at Barua Bamun Gaon, Chargola, Kampur, Cement plant at Bokajan and Badarpur, cosmetics plant of Hindustan Unilever (HUL) at Doom Dooma, etc. Moreover, there are other industries such as jute mill, textile and yarn mills, Assam silk, and silk mills. Many of these industries are facing loss and closure due to lack of infrastructure and improper management practices.

INDUSTRY

Assam is an important producer of silk of different kinds and known for weaving of silk products into saris and fabrics. Production of tusser and other silks and weaving of fabrics is an important occupation for a number of people. Other types of industries are food products, wood and wood products, chemicals and chemical products, non-metallic mineral products. Tea and oil are of prime importance to Assam's economy and also plays a significant role in the economy and life of the state. At Digboy on the border with Burma, Assam has the oldest Indian oil venture and one of the oldest in the world.

In Assam, mining is at present concentrated mainly to four industrial minerals, namely, coal, oil and gas, limestone and sillimanite. The history of coal mining in Assam goes back to the year 1834 when extraction of this mineral on a small scale was being carried out at Cherapunji in upper Assam. Coal was first mined in 1840 near Jaipur by the Assam Tea Co.

But the most important phase in the development of the coal mining industry in Assam was the incorporation of the Assam Railway and Trading Co. in 1882 for the exploitation of the upper Assam coal. The most important coal mines in Assam are situated in the Ledo and Jaipur areas of upper Assam. In the Mikir hills, two small collieries exist -one at Koilajan and other at Seelbhata.

The coal mining activity in the Khasi hills is mostly concentrated around the Laitryngew area. In addition to these small collieries, three mines exist in the Khasi hills. Messrs Thanginath colliery and the Mawsynram colliery are important among them. A small coal mine has been developed at Nangwalbibra in the west Darranggiri Coalfield in the Garo hills under the auspices of the ASMDC, a state government under taking. Petroleum mining is an outstanding feature of Assami's industrial landscape.

Its exploration and development in the state are carried out by the oil and natural gas commission, Oil India Limited and Assam oil company. The discovery of the first oilfield, the Digboy field, goes back to the year 1889. The outstanding work of the BOC in upper Assam has culminated in the discovery of the Nakarkatiya (1953) and Moran (1950) fields which are now developed by the OIL company.

Limestone mining in Assam is confined to surface quarrying. Regular mining activities have been started since 1938 in Therriaghat area in Khasi Hills. Sillimanite has been known to occur at Sonapahar since 1922. In addition to these major minerals, minor minerals such as gravel, sand, building stone and ballast are produced at present at various places in the state.

Assam is endowed with vast mineral resources. The major minerals like coal, oil and gas, limestone, dolomite, sillimanite and corundum, iron ore, felspar, glass-sand, refractory and fire clays, kaolin, beryl, gypsum, pyrite, vermiculite, salt, copper, gold etc. have been reported to occur in the state. The most important minerals being exploited so far in Assam are coal, oil and gas, limestone and sillimanite.

Coal: In Assam, coal occurs in Garo hills, Khasi and Jaintai hills, Mikir hills, Jaipur and Makum. The tertiary coals of Assam are remarkably low in ash but high in sulphur. Assam coal is being consumed at present by the railways, iron and brass foundries, brick kilns, inland water steamer services, tea gardens and other industries in addition to household consumption. Apart from its general uses, Assam coal is eminently suitable for the manufacture of coal distillation products.

Oil and Natural Gas: The oil producing areas of Assam lie in the upper Assam valley and are geologically confined to the Tertiary Strata - mainly Oligocene. Assam is first state in the country where oil was struck in 1889 at Digboy. At present oil is being tapped at two areas - the Digboy and the Naharkotiya and Moran fields. Two more refineries of considerable size have come up in the public sector at Gauhati and Barauni and the third with a petrochemical complex is under way. A new refinery, Numaligarh refinery (3 metric tones capacity) was commissioned on July 9, 1999. The availability of associated natural gas is dependent on the extraction of crude oil. Vast quantities of natural gas are being produced along with the production of crude oil. Only two projects under the "utilization of natural gas scheme" have so far come up in the state. These are the thermal power plant and the fertilizer factory at Namrup.

Limestone: The high-grade fossil limestone or 'nummulitic' limestone deposits of Assam are geologically known as 'Syket limestone' as these belong to that groups of rocks. The limestone deposits are confined in areas of Garo hills, united Khasi and Jaintia hills, Cachar hills and Mikir hills. One of the largest outcrops of limestone is at the foot of the Khasi hills. Vast deposits of high-grade limestone are best observed in the Jowai area. Lime stones of the Khasi and Jaintia hills can be used for manufacture of cement and for lime-burning purposes. It can be used in chemical industries and for metallurgical purposes. The limestone deposits of the state offer vast scope for developing innumerable industries where limestone is required.

Sillimanite: The sillimanite deposits of the Nongstoin state in the Khasi hills are world famous from the point of view of quantity and purity of the mineral. Assam is the major producer of this mineral in India and contributes more than 90% of the total production. Corundum is found to occur in association with the sillimanite deposits. Low-grade 'quartz-sillimanite schists' also occur in the same area.

Clay: Assam is endowed with fairly large reserves of sedimentary white clays as well as Kaolin or 'China clay', which forms an important basic raw material for ceramic or refractory industries. These Clays are found to occur at many places in the Garo hills, Khasi and Jaintia hills and the Mikir hills. This clay is quite suitable for the manufacture of medium to low-grade white wares and other ceramic products like stoneware pipes, sanitary ware, glazed tiles and bricks. The Kaolin deposit near Mawphlang is found to be as good as the Kaolin of corn wall.

Glass Sands: Deposits of fine-grained, white friable sandstones has been located in the coalfields of the Laitryngew and Cherapunji areas. The friable quartzite of the Shilllong series around shillong and the Tura sandstones of the Garo hills are suitable for manufacture of sheet glass and fruit glass after washing.

Iron Ore: Occurrence of banded-iron ore have been located in the Chanderdinga hills and Abhayapuri areas in Goalpara district and in the Aradanga-Rangchapara areas on the border of the Kamrup and Khasi and Jaintia hills districts.

Copper: Copper minerals occur in the Umpyrtha and Ranighat areas in the Khasi and Jaintia hills and also in the Mahamaya hills in Goalpara district.

Felspar: Felspar is a common mineral found to occur in association with granites. Recently workable felspar deposits have been recorded near the Hahim area in Kamrup district.

Gold: Gold is reported to occur in sands, gravels and alluvial terraces along some of the rivers in the Lakhimpur, Sibsagar and Darrang districts of Assam.

A gold-bearing rock was located at a place about 5 miles southwest of Mawphlang.

Gypsum: Gypsum in the form of selenite crystals and disseminated in shale beds occur at Mahendraganj in the Garo hills and at a few places in the Mikir hills.

INDUSTRIAL EXPORT INFRASTRUCTURE

A Software Technology Park has been set up at Guwahati near the Lokapriya Gopinath Bordoloi airport. This park at Guwahati is similar to the ones set up at Noida, Bangalore, Hyderabad and Bhubaneswar by Software Technology Park of India Ltd, a Govt. of India organization.

Export Promotion Industrial Park

Assam Industrial Development Corporation has implemented an Export Promotion Industrial Park (EPIP) at Amingaon near Guwahati in the district of Kamrup at an estimated cost of Rs. 14.62 crores. The Export Promotion Industrial Park has been developed to provide infrastructural facilities of high standard for export oriented units. The basic objectives of EPIP are :

To build and provide industrial infrastructural facilities in an integrated manner. To encourage growth of export oriented industrial units in the state. To sustain the involvement and interest of the state govt. in building and maintain such facilities.

The important features of the EPIP are :

The park will provide developed plots and industrial sheds with power, water, road sewerage and drainage, telecommunication and other requisite facilities.The park is located at Amingaon within Greater Guwahati and adjacent to Inland Container Depot. The Guwahati Airport is 15 kms. away from the site.Allotment of plots will be made to non-polluting industries only.

The total area of the park is 68.10 acres. AIDC has constructed three industrial sheds and allotted to three industrial units. Today, the park has the presence of 37 companies and firms out of which 17 have manufacturing activities.

Food Processing Park

The Government of India has sanctioned a food processing park with a total project cost of Rs. 5.95 crores. The park is being set up near Chaygaon in the district of Kamrup (rural). The implementing agency for the FP is Assam Small Industries Development Corporation Ltd.

Agri Export Zone for Ginger

The Government of India has sanctioned an Agri Export Zone for fresh & processed Ginger for the State in February, 2003. The Nodal Agency for implementing this project is Assam Industrial Development Corporation Ltd.

Industrial Growth Centres

Industrial Growth Centres with high standard infrastructure are being set up at Balipara in Sonitpur district and Matia in Goalpara.

Both the growth centers would have excellent approach and internal roads, dedicated power lines, adequate water supply, communication facilities and central effluent treatment plants in addition to facilities such as banks, post office, fire station, police station etc.

Salient features of the Growth Centre at Matia

Total project cost : Rs. 22.00 croresTotal area : 700 acres (around 450 acres is being proposed to be developed)18 kms. away from the heart of the Goalpara town135 kms. away from the heart of Guwahati city110 kms. from Lokapriya Gopinath Bordoloi (Borjhar) International Airport18 kms. from Goalpara Railway Station

Salient features of the Growth Centre at Balipara

Total Project cost : Rs. 25.44 croresTotal area : 400 acres15 kms. away from heart of the Tezpur town200 kms. from Saloni (Tezpur) Airport7 kms. from Balipara Railway Station2 kms. away from NH - 52.

IID Centre at Bhomoraguri/Naltali, District Nagaon

The Central Government has approved the setting up of an Integrated Infrastructure Development (IID) Centre at Bhomoraguri / Naltali in Nagaon district at a project cost of Rs. 510.00 lakh. The Government land measuring 41 acres has already been taken over. The foundation stone of the project was laid down on 10th January, 2001 and activities for various infrastructure developments are nearing completion.

IID Centre at Dalgaon, District Darrang

The Government of India has approved the setting up of an Integrated Infrastructure Development (IID) Centre at Dalgaon in Darrang District at a project cost of Rs. 418.00 lakh. The Government land measuring 35 acres has already been taken over and the project work in e in progress and nearing completion.

New IID Centres

IID Centre at Demow, District Sivasagar

The Govt. of India has sanctioned a IID Centre at Demow in the Sivasagar District at a cost of Rs. 470.00 lakh. Land measuring 111 Bihgas at Demow has been taken over for the project. The foundation stone for the project has been laid on 23rd July, 2003.

IID Centre at Malinibeel, District Cachar

The Govt. of India has sanctioned another IID Centre at Malinibeel in the District of Cachar. An area of 90 Bighas of land have already been taken over by AIDC for the project. The total cost of the project has been estimated at Rs. 510 lakh.

Proposed IID Centres

Titabor in the district of JorhatRangia in the district of KamrupNorth Lakhimpur in the district of Lakhimpur

Border Trade Centre, Mankachar, District Dhubri

The Govt. of India has approved the setting up of a Border Trade Centre at Mankachar in j Dhubri district at a project cost of Rs. 426.00 lakh. This BTC is going to be implemented by AIDC Ltd.

Border Trade Centre, Sutarkandi, District Karimganj

The Govt. of India has approved the ssetting up of a Border Trade Centre at Sutarkandi in Karimganj district bordering Bangladesh at a project cost of Rs. 8.16 crores. The project is being implemented by Assam Industrial Infrastructure Development Corporation Ltd.

Border Trade Centre, Darranga, District Kamrup

AIDC has prepared a project proposal for establishment of a Border Trade Centre at Darranga bordering Bhutan considering the increasing Border Trade with neighbouring Bhutan. The project cost has been estimated at Rs. 18.00 crores. The project proposal has already been submitted to Govt. of India for its approval.

ECONOMIC INFRASTRUCTURE OF ASSAM

Inland Water Transport

Roads

The major modes of transportation in the state are roads, railways, airways and inland waterways.

Assam state is connected by approximately 69,000 km of road network. The major towns are connected by national highways.

National Highway Length:(in KM) - 2034.24

Airways

There are five civil airports at Guwahati,Tezpur, Jorhat, Dibrugarh, Silchar and North Lakhimpur, There is only one international airport (Loka Priya Gopinath Borodolai International Airport) at Guwahati.

Railways

All the major towns of the state like Dibruharh, Tinsukia, Jorhat, Nagoan, Guwahati, Tezpur, Bangigaon etc are linked with railways. There is approximately 2435 km of railways link across the state.

Waterways

River Brahamaputra and Barak rivers are used as a vast network of waterways. These two rivers effectively fulfill the transport needs of the state.

Routes of Commercial Service

Guwahati-Calcutta-Guwahati, Guwahati-Sirajganj-Guwahati, Guwahati-Narayanganj-Guwahati, Karimganj-Calcutta-Karimganj

The infrastructure development in the State has been slow. It has been lagging behind almost

every State of the country except that of Orissa, Rajasthan, Madhya Pradesh, Himachal Pradesh , Jammu & Kashmir and other North Eastern States.Power generation and distribution is not adequate to support the growth of industry in the State. The conditions of roads and bridges are not at all conducive for promoting any worthwhile economic activity like tourism. These deficiencies in infrastructure have to be attended on priority if economic activities and services are to be supported and encouraged. The power & energy and the following linkages provides on the existing infrastructure in the State.

Power And Energy

Assam possesses immense potential for development of her power sector based on Hydel, Natural gas, Oil and Coal resources.

Assam State Electricity Board was originally constituted on 1st June 1958 in the composite state of Assam under Electricity (Supply) Act, 1948. But the existing ASEB was reconstituted in 1975 when the state of Assam was bifurcated into Assam, Meghalaya and Mizoram. The ASEB is responsible for generation, transmission and distribution of electricity in the state of Assam.

ASEB has six installed projects with the total installed capacity of 574 MW against the peak demand of 621 MW. The power supply position in the state is expected to improve considerably in the coming years with the materialisation of projects under the state sector like Borgolai Thermal Power project (120 MW), Karbi Langpi Project (100 MW) and Amguri Combined Cycle Gas Based project (90 MW).

In the Central sector, NEEPCO has installed and commissioned Kopili HEP (250 MW) and Kathalguri Gas Based Power Project (291 MW). NEEPCO is currently taking up construction of Kopili 2nd stage (25 MW) and it plans to take up the Lower Kopili (150 MW).

7

Tourism

TOURISM IN ASSAM

Roughly shaped like a bird with wings stretching along the length of the Brahmaputra river, Assam is the central state in the North-East Region of India and serves as the gateway to the rest of the Seven Sister States. The land of red river and blue hills, Assam comprises three main geographical areas: the Brahmaputra Valley which constitutes the expansive wingspan, the Barak Valley extending like a tail, and the intervening Karbi Plateau and North Cachar Hills. Assam shares its border with Meghalaya, Arunachal Pradesh, Nagaland, Manipur, Tripura, Mizoram and West Bengal; and there are National Highways leading to their capital cities. It also shares international borders with Bhutan and Bangladesh. In ancient times Assam was known as Pragjyotisha or Pragjyotishpura, and Kamarupa.

6th International Tourism Mart 2017 began in Guwahati on 5 December 2017.

Tourist Hotspots

For the purposes of tourism there are wildlife reserves like the Kaziranga National Park, Manas National Park, Pobitora Wildlife Sanctuary, Nameri National Park, Dibru-Saikhowa National Park etc. It has a rich cultural heritage going back to the Ahom Dynasty which governed the region for many centuries before the British occupation.

A Rhino in Kaziranga National Park

Elephant safari in Kaziranga National Park

A scenic tea estate of Assam

Notable tourist destinations are listed below:

Guwahati

Kamakhya Temple

One of the key urban centres of Assam and the biggest city in North-East India, this serves as the major gateway to the whole region. The major tourist spots of Guwahati are Kamakhya Temple, River Cruise on the river Brahmaputra, Shankardev Kalakshetra, Umananda Temple, Assam State Zoo, Shilpagram etc. Chandubi Lake, Sonapur, Madan Kamdev, Chandrapur and Pobitora Wildlife Sanctuary are other famous spots outskirts the city .While visiting Madan Kamdev Tourists also visit the ancient temple Gopeswar Mandir situated in the village Deuduar.

Majuli

The largest freshwater island in South Asia on the Brahmaputra River. Majuli is famous for its Vaishnavite Satras such as Kamalabari Satra, Dakhinpat Satra, Garamurh Satra, Auniati Satra, Bengenaati Satra and Samaguri Satra.

Kaziranga National Park

This protected area is a UNESCO World Heritage Site and serves as one of the last remaining habitat of the Great Indian One-horned Rhinoceros. Also check out Manas National Park and Orang National Park.

Jatinga

This village is famous for mysterious suicides of the birds, located in Dima Hasao.

Sonitpur

Protected areas to see in the district are Nameri National Park, Bura Chapori Wildlife Sanctuary, Sonai Rupai Wildlife Sanctuary and a part of Orang National Park. Bhalukpong is also an important tourist place. Tezpur is a small town steeped in history and culture. Some of these are Agnigarh, Mahabhairav Temple, Chitralekha Udyan, Bamuni Hills, Usha Pahar etc. Biswanath Chariali town is 75 km away from Tezpur, is famous for the Biswanath Ghat, also called popularly as "Gupta Kashi".

Jorhat

Situated at 318 km east from Guwahati, Jorhat is a very important city, the last capital of Ahom era, as well as the tea capital of India. Important spots in and around Jorhat city are Jorhat Science Centre and Planetarium, Jorhat Gymkhana Club, Raja Maidam, Tocklai Tea Research Institute, Dhekiakhowa Bornamghar, Gibbon Wildlife Sanctuary, Lachit Maidam, Molai forest, Kaziranga Golf Resort, Thengal Bhawan etc.

Sivasagar

Sivadol Temple

As Sivsagar was the seat of the Ahom Kingdom, it is surrounded by many ancient monuments of Ahom era. Those are Rang Ghar, Talatal Ghar, Sivadol, Kareng Ghar of Garhgaon, Joy Dol, Sivasagar Tank, Joysagar Tank, Joymati Maydam, Vishnu Dol, Devi Dol, Gourisagar Dol and Tank, Charaideo, Namdang Stone Bridge etc. Tai Museum and Uttaran Museum which exhibits the history of Ahom. Panidihing Bird Sanctuary, the abode of more than 250 species of birds.

Hajo

Hajo is an ancient pilgrimage centre for three religions Hinduism, Islam and Buddhism.

Haflong

Haflong is the only hill station of Assam. The headquarters of Dima Hasao. The village of Jatinga is known for mysterious bird suicide on the night of new moon.

Tinsukia

Many prominent shopping malls are there in Tinsukia. Dibru-Saikhowa National Park one of the biggest national parks in India are situated in Tinsukia. This national park is considered as one the biological hotspots. The Tilinga Mandir(Bell Temple) is a well-known temple situated in the outskirts of Tinsukia city. Digboi Refinery the Asia's oldest refinery is situated here. A railway park is recent addition to the city. Dehing Patkai Festival annual festival helds at Lekhapani in Tinsukia district. India's only coal museum is situated at Margherita town in Tinsukia district. Tribal communities in Tinsukia district have taken initiatives to promote ecotourism in the region. The Singpho Eco Tourist lodge in Margherita-Pengari road and the Faneng Village at Lekhapani are two such initiatives by the local tribal communities.

Dibrugarh

Dibrugarh is called the tea capital of the world. The town is situated on the edge of the Brahmaputra River. Set amidst extensive tea estates, Dibrugarh offers tourists the opportunity to experience a life in a tea estate. Recently, tea tourism has started becoming popular, with travel companies such as Greener Pastures and Purvi Discovery offering tea tours. Tipam is a famous tourist spot of Dibrugarh. Tipam is an ethnic village which is famous for its historical places. Besides Tipam, Dehing Patkai rainforest is the other attraction. Presently the city has the biggest railway station in Assam with 18 Lines opened in 2009. Rajdhani Express Train Originate from Dibrugarh and Dibrugarh Town.

Practical Information

Weather & Rainfall

Assam has temperate weather with maximum of 35-38 °C in summer and a minimum of 6-8 °C in winter in low-lying areas, particularly the Brahmaputra Valley and Barak Valley. As one ascends towards the hilly areas, however, the mercury falls considerably in winters. Assam experiences high rainfall and humidity – afternoon thunder showers are a common occurrence during monsoons – and early morning fog in winter is also common.

Transportation

Arriving by Air: Guwahati's Lokapriya Gopinath Bordoloi International Airport is well-connected to the major cities in India. Taxi service is including prepaid services are available at the airports for transfer to the city. There are also at Silchar, Dibrugarh, Jorhat and Tezpur which run flights to Kolkata and the other parts of the northeastern region.

Arriving by Rail: The three major routes of the North East Frontier Railway connected Assam to nodal stations in the rest of the country. Guwahati, Assam's largest railway station, is served by direct trains to New Delhi, Kolkata (Saraighat Express), Mumbai (Dadar Express) and Banglore (Banglore Express). There are also direct trains from these cities to Dibrugarh, which is a further 12 hours from Guwahati.

By Road: The Assam State Transport Corporation along with several private companies operates buses connecting Guwahati with Tezpur, Jorhat, Dibrugarh, Tinsukia, Silchar, Dimapur, Kohima, Imphal, Aizawal and Itnagar.

ASSAM TEMPLES AND MONUMENTS

This northeastern state of India is sprawled with numerous temples and monuments, which stand witness to the great historical and cultural past of the state. Some of these monuments date back to the medieval days. This ancestral heritage of the region is preserved in the form of rock sculptures, rock inscriptions, copper plates and other forms of inscriptions hailing from historical to medieval times. Many ancient Hindu temples of Assam have some root in mythological legends. New religions and faiths arriving in this hilly region followed construction of temples and monuments throughout the state. Many of these temples followed architectural styles of the Kachari, Ahom and Kochs. The archeological heritage of Assam has a connection with some of the ancient civilizations of the world. These monuments can be grouped into ancient and modern monuments. Most of the cave temples are dedicated to Lord Shiva, creator of the world as per Hindu belief. The time period of construction of these monuments dates back from 350 AD to 1828 AD. Some of the ancient marvels of Assam are mentioned below -

Kamakhya Temple

Kamakhya Temple is located on top of the Nilachal hill, at a height of around eight hundred feet. It is an ancient Shakti peeth situated in the western part of Guwahati. The goddess Kamakhya is mostly worshipped by Hindus and specially the Tantric worshippers. It is an important pilgrimage centre of Assam. The present day temple was built during the Ahom times. The present structure has preserved the Shikhara characteristic of architecture, which is adorned with beautiful idols of Ganesha and other Hindu gods. The main temple is comprised of three major chambers, rectangular large western chamber, square shaped middle chamber and the narrow eastern chamber. But the most important part is the inner sanatorium or Garbhagraha.

Navagraha Temple

These are devoted to Navagraha or nine celestial bodies according to Hindu astronomy. Some of the temples of South India contain a Navagraha shrine, however Navagraha temples refer to the group of nine temples each dedicated to individual Graha.

The Navgraha temple of Guwahati in Assam was built by Ahom king Rajeshwar Singha during end of 18th Century. The temple was renovated in 1923. It is adorned with nine Shivalingas which are representing the nine Grahas. They are covered with a colored cloth typical of each Graha. A shivalinga in the center represents the presence of Sun.

Umananda Temple

This Shiva temple is beautifully situated on the Peacock Island which is tucked at center of Brahmaputra River in Guwahati. It is located on the mountain called Bhasmacala and it can be accessed by boats from the bank of the river Brahmaputra This temple built by Ahom king Gadadhar Singha a devotee of Shiva, in the period 1681-1696 is dedicated to the presiding deity Umananda. Walls of the temple are decorated with exclusive sculptures and portraits of Hindu gods which are engraved in the rock walls. As per local belief, worshipping this god on Amavasya falling on Monday brings lots of prosperity. A colorful festival is celebrated every year in this temple on Siva Chaturdasi. Hordes of devotees rush to this temple during this festival.

Basisthashram

This is a well known pilgrimage spot located in the southern-most part of Guwahati at the foot hills of Meghalaya. This ashram belonged to the great Vedic sage Bashistha. The region is bedecked by the scenic background of the rivers namely

Sandhya, Lalita and Kanta which meet at this spot offering panoramic views to the visitors.

Mahabhairav Temple

This temple located on a hillock of northern Tezpur was established by king Bana in prehistoric times. This Shiva temple originally built out of stone during Ahom rule, was recently renovated. The temple is popular for its Shivalinga, which is supposed to be the largest in the world. This temple was built in the 8th century by the Salasthamba dynasty. Shivaratri festival is celebrated with great pomp and fervor amidst devotees coming from all corners of the world. The temple can be accessed from Tezpur railway station. It can also be accessed by air, the nearest airport being just seven km from the city center.

Madan Kamdev temple

This temple is tucked on a hillock of Guwahati enriched by Sal and Teak forests, which is dedicated to Lord Kamdev. The temple is stuffed with so many beautiful sculptures, that it has become popular as Khajuraho of Assam. Madan Kamdev is a complex of twenty four temples situated in Kamrup district just thirty five km from Guwahati. The sculptures in the temple are depicting story of Kamdev and his wife Rati. This site is honored as one of the important historical and archeological sites in Assam. Ruined sculpture of Shiva and Parvati is still worshipped by locals but they are known by the name Kamdev and Madan, hence the temple is popular as Madan-Kamdev temple.

Satra

These are institutional centers which follow the Ekasarana tradition, which are independent and controlled by individual adhikaras. Many satras were observed emerging out in the 17th century, which were supported initially by the Koch kingdom and afterwards by Ahom kingdom. These satras proved to be useful in spreading Ekasarana religion. They are housing many bhakals and hold control over their disciples.

Poa Mecca

Poa Mecca means a sect of Mecca which is also called Barmagam, is a Muslim pilgrim center located on the Garurachala Hills. This mosque was built by an Iraqi preacher Ghiyasuddin Auliya in 12th Century AD. The prince turned preacher brought a lump of soil from Mecca and placed it at the spot where the mosque was supposed to be built at a later stage. This place is named as Poa Mecca because a devotee offering prayer at this place, acquires one forth (Poa) spiritual enlightenment compared to what one gets at Mecca.

Da Parbatia

This 6th century architectural marvel in the form of an ancient Hindu temple is located just a few km from the town of Tezpur. On the ruins of this temple, Shiva temple was built during Ahom period which was diminished during the earthquake in Assam leaving only an intact doorframe. This temple preserves some of the finest examples of iconic and sculptural art of Assam. The art style resembles one that existed during Gupta period. Figures of Ganga and Yamuna are carved at the entrance of the temple.

Agnigarh

This is the fortress built by Banasura for keeping his daughter named Usha in isolation. Banasura described in Ramayana was a thousand armed son of Bali and a horrifying demon. Everybody including the gods was afraid of Bana, who was a Shiva follower. The name of the fort is derived from Sanskrit words Agni and Garh. It is located near the banks of river Brahmaputra and is popular as love site of Northeast. Agnigarh literally means residence amidst fire. Once a fortress on a hillock, presently it is a well landscaped garden on the hill with amazing statues to be viewed along its length and breadth.

TOURISM IN NORTH EAST INDIA

Northeast India consists of the eight states Arunachal Pradesh, Assam, Manipur, Meghalaya, Mizoram, Nagaland, Sikkim and Tripura. This article covers tourist attractions in the Northeast region of India.

National parks

- Namdapha National Park - Namdapha National Park is the largest protected area in the Eastern Himalaya biodiversity hotspot and is in Arunachal Pradesh in Northeast India. It is the third largest national park in India in area. It is in the Eastern Himalayan sub-region and is recognized as one of the richest areas in biodiversity in India.
- Kaziranga National Park - Kaziranga National Park is a national park in the Golaghat and Nagaon districts of the state of Assam, India. A World Heritage Site, the park hosts two-thirds of the world's great one-horned rhinoceroses. Kaziranga boasts the highest density of tigers among protected areas in the world and was declared a tiger reserve in 2006.
- Orang National Park - The Orang National Park is on the north bank of the Brahmaputra River in the Darrang and Sonitpur districts of Assam. The park has a rich flora and fauna, including great Indian one-horned rhinoceros, pigmy hog, elephants, wild buffalo and tigers. It is the only stronghold of rhinoceros on the north bank of the Brahmaputra.
- Manas National Park - Manas National Park or Manas Wildlife Sanctuary is a national park, UNESCO Natural World Heritage Site, a Project Tiger reserve, an elephant reserve and a biosphere reserve in Assam.
- Dibru-Saikhowa National Park - Dibru-Saikhowa National Park is a national wildlife park in Tinsukia, Assam. It mainly consists of moist mixed semi-evergreen forests, moist mixed deciduous forests, canebrakes and grasslands. It is the largest salix swamp forest in northeast India.
- Nameri National Park - Nameri National Park is in the foothills of the Eastern Himalayas in the Sonitpur District of Assam. This is excellent elephant country and was considered to be an elephant reserve. It is an ideal habitat for a host of other animals including the tiger, leopard,

sambar, dhole (the Asiatic wild dog), pygmy hog, muntjac, gaur, wild boar, sloth bear, Himalayan black bear, capped langur and Indian giant squirrel.

- Balphakram National Park - Balphakram National Park is a national park about 3,000 metres above sea level, near the Garo Hills in Meghalaya, India. It is often referred to as the "abode of perpetual winds" as well as the "land of spirits." It is the home of the barking deer and the golden cat.
- Nokrek National Park - Nokrek National Park, or Nokrek Biosphere Reserve, is a national park approximately 2 km from Tura Peak in West Garo Hills district of Meghalaya, India. UNESCO added this National park to its list of Biosphere Reserves in May 2009. Along with Balpakram, Nokrek is a hotspot of biodiversity in Meghalaya.

Other national parks

- Mouling National Park is in the Indian state of Arunachal Pradesh.
- Keibul Lamjao National Park is in the Bishnupur district of the state of Manipur.
- Sirohi National Park is located in the state of Manipur.
- Murlen National Park is in the Champhai district Mizoram.
- Ntangki National Park is in Peren district of Nagaland.
- Phawngpui is the Blue Mountain of Mizoram, a highly revered peak, considered to be the abode of the gods. Phawngpui peak is the highest mountain peak in Mizoram.
- Pobitora Wildlife Sanctuary is a wildlife reserve in the Marigaon district of the state of Assam.
- Sipahijola Wildlife Sanctuary is a wildlife sanctuary in Tripura.
- Gorumara National Park is a National Park in northern West Bengal.
- Singalila National Park is located on the Singalila Ridge

at an altitude of more than 7000 feet above sea level, in the Darjeeling district of West Bengal.

- Neora Valley National Park is in the Kalimpong subdivision under Darjeeling District, West Bengal.
- Jaldapara National Park is at the foothills of the Eastern Himalayas in Alipurduar district in West Bengal and on the bank of the Torsa River.

Waterfalls

- Nohkalikai Falls; 1,120 ft Cherapunjee (Meghalaya)
- Nohsngithiang Falls; 1,033 ft (Meghalaya)
- Langshiang Falls – 1,106 ft (Meghalaya)
- Kynrem Falls – 1,001 ft (Meghalaya)
- Elephent Falls (Meghalaya)
- Panimur Falls (Assam)
- Vantawng Falls – 751 ft(Mizoram)
- Nuranang Falls Tawang (Arunachal Pradesh)
- Chmapawati Kunda (Assam)
- Akashiganga Falls (Assam)
- Sivakunda Falls (Assam)
- Bishop Falls (India)(Meghalaya)
- Khaipholangso falls (Karbi Anglong, Assam)
- Belughat falls (Karbi Anglong, Assam)
- Kangthilangso falls (Karbi Anglong, Assam)

Reserved forest

- Kakoijana reserved forest - Kakoijana reserved forest is famous for Golden Langurs.

Hills

- Kangchenjunga - Kangchenjunga is the third highest mountain in the world. It rises with an elevation of 8,586 m (28,169 ft) in a section of the Himalayas called *Kangchenjunga Himal* that is limited in the west by the Tamur River and in the east by the Teesta River. The

Kangchenjunga Himal is located in eastern Nepal and Sikkim, India.

- Naga Hills - The Naga Hills, reaching a height of around 3,825 metres (12,549 feet), lie on the border of India and Burma (Myanmar).
- Patkai Hills - The Patkai hills are on India's northeastern border with Burma.
- Khasi Hills - The Khasi Hills are part of the Garo-Khasi range in the Indian state of Meghalaya, and is part of the Patkai range and of the Meghalaya subtropical forests ecoregion.
- Lushai Hills - The Lushai Hills (or Mizo Hills) are part of the Patkai range in Mizoram and partially in Tripura, India. Hills in Mizoram run north–south. A hill range of the Mizo Poets Square also known as Mizo Hlakungpui Mual runs from north to south. The Poets Square was set up in 1986 to commemorate the Mizo poets and writers at the outskirts of Khawbung. It's one of the most visited sites for tourists.
- Assam Himalaya - Assam Himalaya is a traditional designation for the portion of the Himalaya range between the eastern border of Bhutan, on the west, and the Great Bend of the Tsangpo River, on the east.
- Garo Hills - The Garo Hills are part of the Garo-Khasi range in Meghalaya, India. They are inhabited mainly by tribal dwellers, the majority of whom are Garo people. It is one of the wettest places in the world.
- Sela Pass - Sela Pass is the high-altitude mountain pass in Tawang District of Arunachal Pradesh state of India. It has an elevation of 4,170 m (13,680 ft). It connects the Buddhist city of Tawang Town to Tezpur and Guwahati and is the main road connecting Tawang with the rest of India.

Other hills

- Jongsong Peak is a mountain in the 'Janak' section of the Himalayas. At 7,462 metres (24,482 ft) it is the 57th highest peak in the world, although it is dominated by the third highest, Kangchenjunga, 20 km (12 mi) to the south. Jongsong's summit is at a three-way boundary between Nepal, China and India.

- Gimmigela Chuli, or The Twins, is a mountain in the Himalayas, on the border between Taplejung, Mechi, Nepal and Sikkim, India. It has an elevation of 7,350 m (24,110 ft) above sea level.
- Kabru is a mountain in the Himalayas on the border of eastern Nepal and India. It is part of a ridge that extends south from Kangchenjunga and is the southernmost 7,000 metres (23,000 ft) peak in the world.
- Kirat Chuli or Tent Peak is a mountain in the Himalayas. It lies on the border between Nepal and India.
- Mount Pandim is a Himalayan mountain in Sikkim, India. It has an elevation of 6,691 m (21,952 ft) above sea level.
- Paohanli Peak or Paunhuri is a 7,128-metre-high (23,386 ft) peak at the border of Zarkang, Yadong County, Tibet (China) and Sikkim (India).
- Pauhunri is a mountain in the Eastern Himalayas. It is on the border of Sikkim, India and Tibet, China, and is about 75 km northeast of Kangchenjunga.
- Siniolchu is one of the tallest mountains of the Indian state of Sikkim. The 6,888 metres (22,598 ft) mountain is considered to be particularly aesthetically attractive, having been described by Douglas Freshfield as "the most superb triumph of mountain architecture and the most beautiful snow mountain in the world".

River Islands

- Majuli - Majuli or Majoli is a large river island in the Brahmaputra River, Assam, India, famous for Vaishnavite Satras. The island had a total area of 1,250 square kilometres (483 sq mi). Majuli is the largest river island and the first island district in the Indian subcontinent. It is also recognised by *Guinness Book of World Records* as World's Largest River Island.

- Umananda Island - The Umananda Island, also known as Peacock island, is the home to Umananda temple and it is the smallest inhabited river island in the world.

Hill stations

- Haflong - Haflong is only hills station in Assam, surrounded by lots of natural beauties like fluent water streams, lush green hills and bounty waterfalls.
- Tawang - Tawang town is a town at an elevation of approximately 3,048 metres (10,000 ft) in the northwestern part of Arunachal Pradesh of India.
- Cherrapunji - Cherrapunji is a subdivisional town in the East Khasi Hills district in the Indian state of Meghalaya. It is credited as being the wettest place on Earth, although nearby Mawsynram currently holds that record. Cherrapunji holds the all-time record for the most rainfall in a calendar month and in a year: It received 9,300 mm (370 in) in July 1861 and 26,461 mm (1,041.8 in) between 1 August 1860 and 31 July 1861.

Monasteries

- Pemayangtse Monastery - The Pemayangtse Monastery is a Buddhist monastery in Pemayangtse, near Pelling in the northeastern Indian state of Sikkim, 140 kilometres (87 mi) west of Gangtok.
- Tawang Monastery - Tawang Monastery in the Indian state of Arunachal Pradesh is the largest monastery in India and second largest in the world after the Potala Palace in Lhasa, Tibet.
- Zang Dhok Palri Phodang - Zang Dhok Palri Phodang is a Buddhist monastery in Kalimpong in West Bengal, India. The monastery is atop Durpin Hill, one of the two hills of the town. It was consecrated in 1976 by the visiting Dalai Lama.
- Rumtek Monastery - Rumtek Monastery, also called the "Dharmachakra Centre", is a gompa in the Indian state

of Sikkim near the capital Gangtok. It is a focal point for the sectarian tensions within the Karma Kagyu school of Tibetan Buddhism that characterize the Karmapa controversy.

- Enchey Monastery - Enchey Monastery is in Gangtok, the capital city of Sikkim in the Northeastern Indian state. It belongs to the Nyingma order of Vajrayana Buddhism.
- Tashiding Monastery - Tashiding Monastery is a Buddhist monastery of the Nyingma sect of Tibetan Buddhism in Western Sikkim, northeastern India. It is on top of the hill rising between the Rathong chu and the Rangeet River.
- Dubdi Monastery - Dubdi Monastery, occasionally called 'Yuksom Monastery,' is a Buddhist monastery of the Nyingma sect of Tibetan Buddhism near Yuksom, in the Geyzingsubdivision of West Sikkim district.
- Ralang Monastery - Ralang Monastery is a Buddhist monastery of the Kagyu sect of Tibetan Buddhism in southern Sikkim, northeastern India. It is 6 km from Ravangla.

Lakes

- Khecheopalri Lake - Khecheopalri Lake, originally known as Kha-Chot-Palri (meaning the heaven of Padmasambhava), is a sacred lake for Buddhists and Hindus, which is believed to be a wish-fulfilling lake. It is near Khecheopalri village, 147 kilometres (91 mi) west of Gangtok and 34 kilometres (21 mi) to the northwest of Pelling town in the West Sikkim district of the Northeastern Indian state of Sikkim.
- Gurudongmar Lake - Gurudongmar Lake is one of the highest lakes in the world at an altitude of 17,100 ft (5,210 m). It lies in the district of North Sikkim in the state of Sikkim in India.
- Lake Tsongmo - Lake Tsongmo or Changu Lake is a

glacial lake in the East Sikkim, India, some 40 kilometres (25 mi) from Gangtok at elevation of 3,780 m (12,400 ft).

- Loktak LakeLoktak Lake is the largest freshwater lake in Northeast India is famous for its *phumdis* (heterogeneous decomposing mass of vegetation, soil, and organic matters) floating over it. Keibul Lamjao, the only floating national park in the world, floats over it. It is near Moirang in Manipur state, India.
- Lake Shilloi - The Lake Shillioi is in the district of Phek, Nagaland. Shilloi Lake lies on the lower slopes of the hill ranges running along Myanmar. It is surrounded by beautiful hills. The lake spreads over 0.25 to 0.30 km.
- Umiam Lake - Umiam Lake is a reservoir in the hills 15 km to the north of Shillong in the state of Meghalaya. It is known for its beautiful scenery.

Other lakes

- Chandubi Lake is natural lake in the Kamrup district of Lower Assam 64 km from the city of Guwahati accessible through National Highway 37.
- Dipor Bil, also spelt 'Deepor Beel' (*bil* or *beel* means "lake" in the local Assamese language), is to the southwest of Guwahati city, in Kamrup district of Assam, India.
- Son Beel (Shon Bill) is one of the largest lakes in southern Assam in India. It is situated in the Karimganj district, and is the largest wetland in Assam state.
- Rudrasagar Lake also known as Rudijala, is in Melaghar, Tripura.
- Bijoy sagar is a lake in Udaipur in Eastern India. It is also called Mahadeb Dighi. It is one of the largest lakes in Udaipur in Tripura.

Monuments and other tourist spots

Living root bridges

The living root bridges of Cherrapunji aren't built — they are grown over hundreds of years, in the rainforest of

Cherrapunji. They are alive, growing and gaining strength over time.They are also present in Laitkynsew, and Nongriat.

Madan Kamdev

Madan Kamdev is a famous archaeological site in Kamrup district of Assam. This site has ruins of huge and small temples scattered around an old temple of Lord Shiva: Gopeshwar Temple is near a village and a big cave nearby is known as Parvati Guha.

Meghalaya Caves

The Indian state of Meghalaya is famous for its many caves, which attract tourists from India and abroad. A few of the caves in this region have been listed amongst the longest and deepest in the world. A famous one is Mawsmai caves near Cherrapunji are the limestone caves, lies near the village of Mawsmai. Meghalaya is famous in the world for its deep caves such as the Siju Cave; Krem Liat Prah is the longest cave in Asia.

Capital cities

Agartala

Agartala is capital of Tripura state. Its second largest city in Northeast India after Guwahati. Places of attraction in Agaratala:

- College Tilla — Maharaja Bir Bikram College, Tripura University buildings, football ground, international cricket stadium, picturesque lush landscapes and serene natural lakes. It is also a National Bird Sanctuary.
- Ujjayanta Palace — Palace of the Tripura kings, was converted to state legislative assembly and is now into a museum; in the area of Palace Compound is one of the eye-catching attraction in the state.
- Jagannath temple — Hindu temple of Vaishnava school of thought. It has been transformed into the Ujjayanta Museum and it was inaugurated by Dr. Hamid Ansari, the vice president of India.

- Umamaheswar temple — Hindu temple of Shaiva and Shakti(durga).
- Venuban Buddha Vihar — Around 2 km inside the city of Agartala from the city center is the Venuban Vihar where a Buddha shrine houses a metal idol of Lord Buddha.
- Krishna Mandir
- Puratan Agartala (Old Agartala)
- Malancha Niwas — Rabindranath Tagore, the first Asian Nobel Laurete had stayed here during his visit to Tripura.
- Agartala Amusement Park, Amtali- Chocolate Hotels Pvt Ltd
- Agartala City Centre — The main hub point in the city, in Paradise Chowmuhuni, carries a lot of attraction in the capital.
- Agartala Secretariat — Approximately 3 km from the heart of the city, this is a splendid place to watch the biggest government building in Northeast India.
- Rabindra Kanan
- Nehru Park
- Heritage Park
- Tripura State Museum is at the Ujjayanta Palace.
- Science Museum, in Sukanta Academy.
- Haveli Museum, in Kashipur.

Aizawl

Aizawl is the capital of Mizoram state. The main places of interest in Aizawl are:

- Bara Bazar is the main shopping centre of Aizawl in Dawrpui Veng locality. The steep Zion Street is lined with stalls selling garments. The main bazar is where the people are best seen in their traditional costumes selling produce from the farms as well as imports from China brought through Myanmar. The Millennium Centre in the same locality is a popular shopping mall.

- Mizoram State Museum is in the centre of the town at Zarkawt. This museum gives a good insight into Mizo traditions, culture and history.
- Reiek Tourist Resort, a tourist spot 12 km from Aizawl, is a beautiful place at an elevation of 1548 metres with a traditional Mizo village.
- Durtlang Hills on the northern side of Aizawl offers a fine view of the hill station from Durtlang Hospital or Aizawl Theological College.
- Hmuifang is about 50 km from Aizawl with an elevation of 1619 metres. The mountain is covered with virgin forests reserved since the Mizo chief's time.
- Berawtlang Tourist Complex 7 km from Aizawl is a recreational centre that hosts cultural activities. It is considered a popular picnic spot.
- Baktawng Village, 70 km from Aizawl, is where Pu Ziona lives with the "worlds largest existing family" with 39 wives, 94 children, 14 daughters-in-law and 33 grandchildren.
- Solomon's Temple, Aizawl Mizoram, India in Kidron Valley, Chawlhhmun is a grand temple complex operated by Kohhran Thianghlim of Mizoram.
- Khuangchera Puk is a cave in Ailawng near Reiek, about 30 km from Aizawl.

A panorama of Aizawl taken from Zemabawk.

Gangtok

Gangtok is the capital of Sikkim state. City is known for its tourist attractions.

Guwahati

Guwahati is the commercial capital of Assam state and its largest city in North East India.

- River cruise: One of the major attractions of Guwahati is the cruise on the Brahmaputra river. On board these luxurious cruise vessels tourists can relax and enjoy the beautiful view of the sunset.
- Umananda Temple: On the Peacock Island in the middle of the Brahmaputra, this Shiva temple was built in 1664. It is believed that Lord Shiva by using his third eye burnt Kamdeva here. Every year Shivaratri is celebrated in this temple in a great way. The island is believed to be the world's smallest human inhabited island. The world's largest river island is Majuli.
- Accoland: Accoland family fun kingdom is the northeast's only amusement park named after Acco, the mythological king of amusement. This park is at Patgaon.
- Srimanta Sankaradeva Kalakshetra: Shankardev Khalakshetra's name is synonymous with the Vaishnava saint and scholar of Assam Srimanta Shankardeva. It is a multipurpose cultural complex that has fulfilled its aim in protecting, promoting and preserving the cultural heritage of the communities and tribes of Assam and the country.
- Guwahati Planetarium: In Uzanbazar this planetarium is the only one of its kind in the northeastern region and a center of astronomical research. For visitors, the mysterious aspects of the universe are brought alive by sheer audio-video technique and explained in the dark domed structure inside the planetarium.
- Assam State Museum: Assam State Museum is near Dighalipukhuri. It houses many rare, specimen of the

Ahom Dynasty. Many articles of equipment, dress materials belonging to the glorious past of Assam are found here. Many antiques, statues, manuscripts, written on Shashi-paat and other valuable articles are preserved and displayed.

- Kamakhya Temple: Kamakhya Temple, some 5 km from the main city on the Nilachal Hill, is one of the most sacred Hindu shrines of India. Goddess Kamakhya is worshipped here. Ambubachi Mela is celebrated every year in the middle of June in this temple. Many devotees from across the country gathered here during this mela.
- Shilpagram: Adjacent to Srimanta Shankardev Kalakshetra, this is the only crafts village of the North East Zone Cultural Center (NEZCC). It had made landmark in the promotion of the varied arts and cultures of the local people. It holds regular cultural events throughout the year in its open air stage and auditorium.
- Nehru Park: At heart of the city at Panbazar by the side of Cotton College. The highlights of the park are the concrete statues of Bihu dance, Ojapali dance, Deodhani dance, Jhumur dance, Bhoor tal dance etc. There are altogether 45 concrete statues depicting these aspects of Assamese life and culture.
- NEDFi Haat: NEDFi Haat is at a leased building of Industries & Commerce Department Govt. of Assam. In NEDFi Haat visitors can buy handicraft and handloom products. They can buy traditional food items produced by the self-help groups of the state in the Bihu seasons.
- Assam State Zoo cum Botanical Garden: Assam State Zoo cum Botanical Garden is the largest zoo of the northeast at Hengerabari Reserved Forest in the city.
- Basistha Temple: Basistha Temple is on Sandhyachal Hill, on the southern part of the city; this beautiful tourist spot was once the ashram (hermitage) of sage Basistha.
- Sukreswar Temple: Sukreswar Temple is an ancient Shiva temple built by Ahom king Pramatta Singha on Dakini Jogini hill by the side of river Brahmaputra.

- Navagraha Temple: Navagraha temple or temple of nine planets is on Chitrachal Hill to the east. It was the ancient seat of study of astronomy and astrology. The nine planets are represented by the nine linga's inside the main temple. There is a stone imprint of solar system inside the temple. This temple is 3 km from the railway station is a center of Astrological and Astronomical research. It was for this temple Guwahati was named Pragjyotishpura.
- Dighalipukhuri: At the heart of the city at Uzanbazar and surrounded by the High Court on the north and the State Museum and District Library on the south. This is a huge man-made tank. It was excavated by King Bhagadatta to celebrate the 'swayambar' of his daughter Bhanumati who was married to Kourava prince Druyadhana. There is a boating club on the Dighalipukhuri.
- Ugro Tara Temple: At the heart of the city banks of Joarpukhuri (twin ponds). The Ugro Tara Temple is another shakti peeth temple where the eyes of sati were believed to have fallen.
- Balaji Temple, Guwahati: This temple is a recent addition to the religious places of Guwahati. It is at Betkuchi area of the city. Balaji temple with striking South Indian architecture is unlike the other temples of this place. In the evening the temple is illuminated by electric lights.
- ISKCON Temple, Guwahati: This temple belongs to the ISKCON society founded by Abhay Charanaravinda Bhaktivedanta Swami Prabhupada. The temple's main deity is Radha-Krishna. The main emphasis of this temple's preaching lies on the teachings of Krishna and Bhagavad Gita.
- Madan Kamdev & Gopeshwar Mandir is near to Guwahati in a village named as Deuduar.
- Northbrook Gate: It was constructed to welcome British viceroy Lord Northbrook who visited Guwahati in 1874

near Sukreswar Ghat. British officials named it 'Gateway of Assam'.

- North East Crafts Museum and Showroom of Handicrafts & Handlooms: An undertaking of North Eastern Handicrafts and Handlooms Development Corporation Limited (a Govt. of India Enterprise) this showroom has a wide variety of bamboo and cane handicrafts from across the Northeast India. Visitors can buy these indigenous handicraft products from the showroom. The showroom is in Garchuk in Guwahati.

Panoramic view of Guwahati City.

Imphal

Imphal is capital of Manipur state. Some of the places of attractions in city as follows.

- Kangla Palace: It is on both sides (western and eastern) of the bank of the Imphal River. It was the traditional seat of the past Meitei rulers of Manipur.
- Hiyangthang Lairembi Temple Complex: A religious site and a tourist attraction, the temple complex is noted for its annual Durga Puja festival in September or October.
- Imphal War Cemetery: This cemetery remembers British and Indian soldiers who fought and died in the Second World War (1944).
- Women's Market (*Ima Keithel*): The market stalls are all run by women, and it is reportedly the only such market in the world.

- Jama Masjid: A holy place for Muslims in Imphal, it is the only mosque in the Imphal market (on the bank of the Nambul River).
- Shree Govindajee Temple: The temple was considered the apex of cultural activity during the reign of the Maharajas. Near the palace, it has two domes and a raised congregation hall.
- ISKCON Temple: The ISKCON Temple is near the road from Imphal Airport to the city.

Itanagar

Itanagar is the capital of Arunachal Pradesh. Major tourist sites include:

- Ita Fort: Ita Fort in Itanagar town is one of the most important historical sites in the state of Arunachal Pradesh, India. The name literally means "Fort of bricks" (brick being called "ita" in the Ahom language).
- Jawaharlal Nehru Museum, Itanagar: Known for showcasing tribal culture of the state.
- Ganga Lake is a beautiful natural lake locally known as Gekar Sinyi (Confined water in the Nyishi dialect) surrounded by a landmass of hard rock. Primeval vegetation, orchids masses on tall trees and tree ferns contribute to its popularity as a picnic spot. Boating facilities and a swimming pool are available at the site.

Kohima

Kohima is the capital of Nagaland. The city is known for its Hornbill Festival. Major tourist sites include:

- War Cemetery is a memorial dedicated to the soldiers of the 2nd British Division of the Allied Forces who died in the Second World War at Kohima, in April 1944.
- Naga Heritage Village is a vista of nature, cheerful and hospitality of people. The Heritage Village protects and preserves all ethnic cultural heritages of Nagaland. It upholds and sustains the unique identity of dialects,

customs and traditions of all the ethnological tribes of Nagaland.

Shillong

Shillong is the capital of Meghalaya.

Places of interest in and around Shillong includes:

- Elephant Falls: 12 km on the outskirts of the city, the mountain stream descends through two successive falls set in dells of fern covered rocks.
- Lady Hydari Park: The park stretches over a kilometre and has an adjacent mini zoo.
- Wards Lake: Known locally as Nan-Polok, it is an artificial lake with garden and boating facilities.
- Shillong Golf Course: Shillong has one of the largest golf courses (the world's wettest) in Asia: Gleneagles of the East. It enjoys the rare distinction of being one of the few natural golf courses in Asia. Not only is the Shillong Golf Course scenic and enjoyable, it is also challenging. A group of British civil service officers introduced golf to Shillong in 1898 by constructing a nine-hole course. The present 18-hole course was inaugurated in 1924. The course is set in a valley covered with pine and rhododendron trees. The tight fairways, carpeted with a local grass which hardens the soil, are difficult to negotiate. The number of out-of-bounds streams that criss-cross every fairway makes it all the more trying. Obstructions come in the form of bunkers, trees and rain. The longest hole is the 6th, which is a grueling 594 yards. Shillong Golf Course is considered to be the "Glen Eagle of the East" at the United States Golf Association Museum. It was set in a valley at an altitude of 5200 ft in 1898 as a nine-hole course and later converted into an 18-hole course in 1924 by Captain Jackson and C. K. Rhodes.
- Motphran: The "Stone of France" which is locally known as "Motphran" was erected in memory of the 26th Khasi Labour Corps who served under the British in France

during World War I. It bears the words of the famous Latin poet Horace "Dulce et decorum est pro patria mori" which can be roughly translated as "It is sweet and fitting to die for one's country."

- Shillong Peak: A picnic spot, 10 km from the city, 1965 m above sea level, offers a panoramic view of the scenic countryside and is the highest point in the state. Obeisance is paid to U Shulong at the sanctum sanctorum at the peak's summit every springtime, by the religious priest of Mylliem State.
- Capt. Williamson Sangma State Museum: For those interested in ethnic tribal culture and tradition this government museum offers insights to the lifestyle of the people. This museum is in the State Central Library complex where monuments for the great patriots of the state were erected besides the statue of Smt. Indira Gandhi and Netaji Subhash Chandra Bose.
- Don Bosco Centre for Indigenous Cultures: The Don Bosco Museum is part of DBCIC (Don Bosco Centre for Indigenous Cultures). DBCIC comprises research on cultures, publications, training, animation programmes and the museum, which is a place of knowledge-sharing on the cultures of the northeast in particular, and of culture in general. DBCIC with its Don Bosco Museum is at Mawlai, Shillong.
- Entomological Museum (Butterfly Museum): A privately owned museum of M/s Wankhar, Riatsamthiah, Shillong about 2 km from Police Bazar is the only known museum in India devoted to moths and butterflies.
- Air Force Museum at Upper Shillong
- Forest Museum in Lady Hydari Park
- Rhino Heritage Museum at Shillong
- Zoological Museum in Risa Colony
- Anthropological museum at Mawblei
- Botanical Museum at 4th Furlong

- Arunachal Museum at the Cantonment Area
- Chrysalis the Gallery: This art gallery is on the second floor of Salonsar Mansion at Police Bazaar, the commercial hub of Shillong. Chrysalis has flexible spacing to display paintings (canvases), sculpture, photography and handicrafts. Run by a local artist, Jaya Kalra, the gallery caters to exhibitions of artists and artisans especially from the northeast and also from the rest of India.
- State Museum: Located at the State Central Library complex.
- Cathedral of Mary Help of Christians is in Don Bosco Square.
- Bishop and Beadon Falls: Both cascade down the same escarpment into a deep valley.
- Spread Eagle Falls: 3 km from Polo Grounds.
- Sweet Falls: Sweet Falls (also called "Weitden," in the native dialect) is the most beautiful of all the waterfalls in Shillong. It lies about 5 km from the Happy Valley and is about 96 m in height.
- Crinoline Falls: Near Lady Hydari Park.
- Madina Masjid: The only glass mosque in India. Madina mosque is the rare architectural marvel in India as it has an striking and glittering structure of glass.

ASSAM WILDLIFE

Pobitora Wildlife Sanctuary

State: Assam in the north eastern state of India.

Best time to Travel: November to March.

Location: Pobitora Wildlife Sanctuary in Assam is about 50 km from the Guwahati, the commercial capital of Assam.

Know the Pobitora Wildlife Sanctuary: Pobitora Wildlife Sanctuary is major wildlife stock, situated in Morigaon district of Assam, the northeastern state of India. Covering an area of 38.8 sq. km., the Pobitora Wildlife Sanctuary is about 50 km from Guwahati, situated on the border of Nagaon and Kamrup Distt.

Pobitora is mainly famous for its great Indian one horned Rhinoceros. Besides Rhinoceros the other animals are Asiatic Buffalo, Leopard, Wild bear, civet cat etc. Assam Pobitora Wildlife Sanctuary is also home to more than 2000 migratory birds and various reptiles.

Journey to the Pobitora Wildlife Sanctuary

Airport: The nearest Airport to the wildlife sanctuary is Guwahati.

Railhead: Guwahati is well-connected to all the major cities of the country by rail. One can easily reach the park by bus or other vehicles from the Guwahati railhead.

Road Transport: Guwahati can be accessed by road from any part of Assam. Once in Guwahati, you can easily reach the park by any means of road transport.

Staying near the Pobitora Wildlife Sanctuary

Guwahati offers several private hotels ranging from luxury to budget-friendly ones. Fish is a major delicacy in Assam and one can savour mouthwatering curries in and around Paltan Bazar at cheap rates. There are excellent accommodation facilities in and around Guwahati in Assam.

Kaziranga National park

State: Assam in India.

Best time to Travel: November to April.

Weather Conditions: Climate Temp. Summer Max 35 C Min. 18 C. Winter Max 24 C Min 7 C. Annual rainfall 2300 mm, heavy in summer.

Location: The National Highway 37 runs through the park. Kaziranga (Kohora) is at a distance of 217 km from Guwahati, 96 km from Jorhat, and 75 km from Furkating via road.

Know the Kaziranga National Park: Located in the heart of Assam on the bank of the majestic Brahmaputra is the Kaziranga National Park. Kaziranga National Prak in Assam is inhabited by the world's largest population of one-horned rhinoceroses, as well as many mammals, including tigers, elephants, panthers and bears, and thousands of birds.

Assam Kaziranga National Park covers an area of approximately 430-sq-kms with its swamps and tall thickets of elephant grass making it the most ideal habitat for the one-horned Indian Rhino. Due to countless poaching of this prehistoric survivor, the Kaziranga National Park was declared a wildlife sanctuary in 1940.

Park Speciality

Kaziranga National Park is the only national park reserve in India where the rhinoceros can be seen in its natural habitat.

Journey to Kaziranga National Park

Airport: The nearest airport is situated at Guwahati, which is 217-km away from the park. The other airport is located at Jorhat, 96-km from Kaziranga.

Railhead: The nearest railhead is Furkating, situated 75-km away from Kaziranga National Park.

Road Tansport: The main gate for Kaziranga Wildlife Sanctuary, at Kohora on the NH-37, consists of a handful of cafes and a small local market. ASTC and private buses stop here on their way to and from Guwahati, Tezpur and Upper Assam. Some private buses also retain a seat quota for Kaziranga passengers.

Staying near Kaziranga National Park : Most of the accommodation available at the park is located along the NH 37, which runs along the southern border of the park. The main locations of accommodation facilities are at Kohora and Baguri. There is a variety of accommodation types to choose from which consist of Forest rest houses, Bungalows, Lodges and Hotels. Even though the number of rooms available is good, the demand is more than the supply and it is advisable to make your bookings well in advance to avoid last minute harassment.

The Ecosystem of the Park

The Landscape: The land is quite level all over the park, which is mostly covered by dense and tall elephant grass. These large stretches of elephant grass are intermixed by small wetlands left behind by the receding floodwaters of the river Brahmaputra. The park, although quite flat in nature, is set against a backdrop of hills like the Mikir and Karbi Anglong.

The Flora: These picturesque wetlands have an abundant cover of water lilies, water hyacinth and lotus. The vegetation that breaks the monotony of these grasslands are large clumps of semi-evergreen forest. The park is mostly covered with elephant size grass, making it a perfect habitation for the one-horned rhinos.

The Fauna: Indian One-horned Rhinos (900), tigers (50), leopards (20), elephants (700), barasingha or swamp deer (700), barking deer (300), wild boar (700), para or hog deer (7000), Bison (22), Sambar (400), leopard cats, otters (300), Hoolock Gibbons, golden Langurs, Wild Buffaloes (600), Slow Loris, pygmy hog, capped langur and bears (50).

Note: The numbers provided here are approximate figures taken from the park's census findings in the 1990s.

The Birds: Grey headed fishing eagle, Pallas' fishing eagle, Crested serpent eagle, Swamp partridge, Red jungle fowl, Bengal floricab, Bar headed goose, Whistling Teal, Pelicans, Rose breasted Parakeets, Black necked Storks, Adjutant Storks, Open Billed Storks, Egrets, Herons and White wired wood ducks are among the major number of bird varieties visible in the parks.

The Reptiles: Rock Pythons and many more varieties of snakes, Monitor Lizards and Turtles are abundant in the park.

Trip within the Kaziranga National Park: It is possible to tour the park interiors on the back of one of two available modes of transport. The modes - Elephant and Jeep.

Elephant Rides: The first and more preferred mode is on elephant's back. Elephant rides allow you to get up very close to the wild animals and make you feel totally one with nature due to the lack of any sound of an engine.

These rides are taken out thrice in a day from Mihimukh, which is located 3 km from Kohora. There are only around 5 elephants available for touring purposes and it is definitely advisable to book your ride well in advance. These advance bookings can be made at the Bonani Lodge at Kohora.

Jeep Safaris: Jeep Safaris are also available and can be booked at the various lodges and through local operators.

Manas National Park

State: Assam in North East India.

Best Time to Travel: November to April.

Location: The Manas National Park is located at a distance of 176 km from Guwahati. It is about 41 km from the Barpeta road.

Know the Manas National Park: Manas National Park in Assam is situated on the foothills of the Himalayas and a part of it continues across the international border into Bhutan, where it is known as the Royal Manas National Park. Covering an area of 391 sq. km, the Manas National Park was declared a sanctuary on 1st of October, 1928 and was designated a World Heritage site in December 1985.

The Assam Manas National Park with its picturesque beauty and incomparable wealth of wildlife offers one of the most enthralling experiences. The sanctuary also a world heritage site is home to a great variety of wildlife, including tiger, golden langur, wild buffalo, hispid hare, pigmy hog, capped langur, Indian one-horned rhinoceros, elephant, gaur, hog deer, etc.

Park Speciality

Manas known for its Project Tigers, Rhinos & Elephants, and is Assam's one of the two Tiger projects.

Journey to the Manas National Park

Airport: Manas Park is 176-kms from Guwahati. The nearest airport is Borjhar, which is situated, 5-km out of town, and can be reached by rickshaw, auto rickshaw or airline buses.

Railhead: The nearest railhead is situated at Barpeta road.

Road Transport: Buses regularly ply from Guwahati to Barpeta Road in 4½ hrs.

Staying near the Manas National Park: The only accommodation facilities available inside the park are two bungalows at Mathanguri. There are no arrangements here for catering and all rations should be carried in with you.

Other than the bungalows at Mathanguri inside the park, tourist lodges are available at Barpeta Road and Bansbari. Food is not a problem here and they are located an hour's drive from the park. The facilities offered are pretty basic and the charges are quite economical.

The Park Ecosystem

The Landscape: The landscape of the park is mostly small grasslands located between the densely forested foothills with many rivulets, streams and natural drains flowing all over. In the lower regions, there are many smooth sandy belts with clumps of trees growing in and around them. In general, Manas National Park in Assam offers some of the most pleasing natural surroundings in the country.

The Flora: The vegetation that covers most of the park is of the mixed deciduous variety. This mixed forest is interspersed by small glades of grass where deer can be seen grazing in large numbers.

The Fauna: The animal population of Manas is very excitingly diverse. Some of the more fierce or potentially aggressive creatures it shelters within it's region are Tigers, Elephants, Rhinos, Wild Buffaloes, Leopards, Clouded Leopards and the rare Black Panthers.

The park is also a haven for 22 highly endangered species of Hispid Hare and the Pygmy Hog.

Some of the other animals sighted while exploring the park are Gaurs, Swamp Deer, Capped Langurs, Golden Langurs, Assamese Macaques, Slow Loris, Hoolock Gibbons, Smooth Indian Otters, Sloth Bears, Barking Deer, Hog Deer, Sambar and Chital.

The Birds: Assam Manas National Park is a favourite with many bird species, both resident and migratory. Some of these are Giant Hornbills, Jungle Fowls, Bulbuls, Brahminy Ducks, Khaleej Pheasants, Egrets, Pelicans, Fishing Eagles, Serpent Eagles, Falcons, Scarlet Minivets, Bee-Eaters, Magpie Robins, Pied Hornbills, Gray Hornbills, Mergansers, Harriers, Ospreys and Herons.

Trip within the Manas National Park

Jeep Safaris: The ideal way to view most part of the park is in a 4-wheel drive petrol vehicle. This will get you to each of the parts without being too noisy.

Boat Rides: These boats rides are best for viewing animals like the wild buffaloes. Some of the animals that comes out on the banks of the river Manas can be seen from the safety and serenity of a boat which commences its ride from Mathanguri and ends around 35 km away, from where one is picked up by pre-arranged transport.

Elephant Rides: The most favourite of all is the elephant rides organised by the park authorities from Mathanguri. These take you deep in to the remote areas of the forest and often ride in between some of the wildlife there, including elephants, rhinos and wild buffaloes.

8

Population and Religion

POPULATION OF ASSAM 2018

Assam is a state situated in the northeastern side of India. Assam contains the Brahmaputra Valley, Karbi Anglong and Dima Hasao locales. Assam is one of the Seven Sister States of Northeast India and it is located in the southern part of the East Himalayas.

The state is popular all over the globe for Assam tea and Assam silk. The first ever oil well in Asia was entered here. It has proportioned the one-horned Indian rhinoceros from close eradication and also the wild water buffalo, tiger and diverse sorts of Asiatic feathered creatures. The state offers one of the last wild living spaces for the Asian elephant.

Population Of Assam In 2018

The total population of the state was 26.66 million with 4.91 million family units in 2001. Higher population fixation was recorded in the areas of Kamrup, Nagaon, Barpeta and Cachar. The population was assessed at 28.67 million in the year 2006, 30.57 million in 2011 and is expected to achieve 34.18 million by 2021 and 35.60 million by the year 2026.

Talking about population, in order to check out the population of Assam in 2018, we need to have a look at the population of the past 5 years. They are as per the following:

1. 2013 – 31.86 Million
2. 2014 – 32.28 Million
3. 2015 – 33.41 Million
4. 2016 – 33.90 Million
5. 2017 – 34.492 Million

Predicting the 2018 population of Assam is not easy but we can get the idea after analysing the population from the year 2013 – 17. As we have seen that every year the population increases by approximate 0.5264 Million people. Hence, the population of Assam in 2018 is forecast to be 34,492 Million + 0.5264 Million = 35.0184 Million. So, the population of Assam in the year 2018 as per estimated data is 35.0184 Million.

Assam Population 2018 –35.0184 Million. (estimated).

Demography Of Assam

The Assamese Hindus are the greatest community in the state. The number of Assamese Hindus in this state is 11,379,000, containing 36.50% of the state's population at 2011 assessment. (69%) separate themselves provincially, 22 locally and around 3 trans-broadly. The early pioneers were Austroasiatic and Dravidians speakers, followed by Indo-Aryan speakers, Tibeto-Burman. Forty-five languages are spoken by different gatherings, including three important dialect families.

Population Density And Growth Of Assam

The population density of the state of Assam is 497 persons per square kilometre. While the number of inhabitants in India rose to 1.21 billion people over the span of the current 10 years and there has been a growth of 181 million as demonstrated by the new enrolment, the insights report revealed a couple of attributes in the check and features population of the territory of Assam.

While Dhubri recorded the highest population growth, it waited behind with respect to growth and proficiency. Yet again, female populace outperformed that of the males in the state. Augmentation in education among females moreover came as a pleasant shock. There has been a mind blowing growth rate of Assam in the recent years and it is going on.

Facts About Assam:

1. Assam is famously known for its Tea. Assam is the biggest tea delivering state in the nation, accounting to pretty much 50 percent of the total generation.
2. Assam is moreover known for wildlife sanctuaries and national parks. Assam has been successful in sparing various wild lives from extinction. Popular wildlife spots in Assam are Kaziranga National Park, Deepor Beel Bird Sanctuary, Nambor Wildlife Sanctuary and others.
3. The noteworthy conduits of Assam are Brahmaputra and Barak stream.
4. Assam has a tropical rainstorm climate. It witnesses significant precipitation and the summer temperature remains within 38 degree Celsius.
5. The primary oil reserves of the nation were found in Assam in the late nineteenth Century and that is one of the reasons Assam is one of the broad and old petroleum assets.

DEMOGRAPHICS – POPULATION

The total population of Assam was 26.66 million with 4.91 million households in 2001. Higher population concentration was recorded in the districts of Kamrup, Nagaon, Sonitpur, Barpeta, Dhubri, Darrang, and Cachar. Assam's population was estimated at 28.67 million in 2006 and at 30.57 million in 2011 and is expected to reach 34.18 million by 2021 and 35.60 million by 2026.

As per the 2011 census, the total population of Assam was 31,169,272. The total population of the state has increased from 26,638,407 to 31,169,272 in the last ten years with a growth rate of 16.93%.

Of the 32 districts, eight districts registered a rise in the decadal population growth rate. Religious minority-dominated districts like Dhubri, Goalpara, Barpeta, Morigaon, Nagaon, and Hailakandi, recorded growth rates ranging from 20 per cent to 24 per cent during the last decade. Eastern Assamese districts, including Sivasagar and Jorhat, registered around 9 per cent population growth. These districts do not have any international border.

In 2011, the literacy rate in the state was 73.18%. The male literacy rate was 78.81% and the female literacy rate was 67.27%. In 2001, the census had recorded literacy in Assam at 63.3% with male literacy at 71.3% and female at 54.6%. The urbanisation rate was recorded at 12.9%.

The growth of population in Assam has increased since the middle decades of the 20th century. The population grew from 3.29 million in 1901 to 6.70 million in 1941. It increased to 14.63 million in 1971 and 22.41 million in 1991. The growth in the western and southern districts was high primarily due to the influx of people from East Pakistan, now Bangladesh.

The mistrust and clashes between Indigenous Assamese people and Bengali Muslims started as early as 1952, but is rooted in anti Bengali sentiments of the 1940s. At least 77 people died and 400,000 people was displaced in the 2012 Assam violence between indigenous Bodos and Bengali Muslims.

The People of India project has studied 115 of the ethnic groups in Assam. 79 (69%) identify themselves regionally, 22 (19%) locally, and 3 trans-nationally. The earliest settlers were Austroasiatic speakers, followed by Tibeto-Burman, Indo-Aryan speakers, and Tai–Kadai speakers. Forty-five languages are spoken by different communities, including three major language families: Austroasiatic (5), Sino-Tibetan (24) and Indo-European (12). Three of the spoken languages do not fall in these families. There is a high degree of bilingualism.

RELIGIONS

Religion in Assam (2011)

Hinduism (61.47%)

Islam (34.22%)

Christianity (3.7%)

Buddhism (0.2%)

Jainism (0.01%)

Sikhism (0.01%)

Animism (0.01%)

Other or not religious (0.3%)

According to the 2011 census, 61.47% were Hindus, 34.22% were Muslims. Christian minorities (3.7%) are found among the Scheduled Tribe population. The scheduled Tribe population in Assam is around 13%, of which Bodos account for 40%. Other religions followed include Jainism (0.1%), Buddhism (0.2%), Sikhism (0.1%) and Animism (amongst Khamti, Phake, Aiton etc. communities). Many Hindus in Assam are followers of the Ekasarana Dharma sect of Hinduism, which gave rise to Namghar, designed to be simpler places of worship than traditional Hindu temples.

Out of 32 districts of Assam, 9 are Muslim majority according to the 2011 census of India. The districts are Dhubri, Goalpara, Barpeta, Morigaon, Nagaon, Karimganj, Hailakandi, Darrang and Bongaigaon.

RELIGIOUS PLACES

Assam has several important temples, making the sites very important to the sacred geography of Hinduism, and this includes:

The Kamakhya Temple is situated near Guwahati in Assam. It is revered as one of the Shakti Peethas, and is visited by thousands throughout the year. It is also the focus of many myths, stories, and historical events.

The Kachakanti Temple in Udharbond, near Silchar is one of the most respected places of worship for Hindus in Assam.

The Surya Pahar Temple: It is situated in Goalpara district in Assam. It is an ancient centre of sun worship and there are numerous insufficiently explored archaeological remains around it.

The Navagraha Temple: It is situated on the Chitrasal or Navagraha hill in Guwahati. The temple is famous for its unique feature of planetary faith.

Sivadol, a Shiva Temple, situated in Sivasagar city is an another religious place where thousands of Shiva devoters come daily.

Besides these, other Devi Dol and Vishnu Dol (Temple) are also located to fulfill the desire of devotees and these temples were built by earlier Ahom Kings. There are also the Uma Nanda Temple located on the Peacock island in middle of River Brahmaputra in Guwahati, the Mahabhairav Temple in Tezpur and the Rangnath Dol in Joysagar. These are important Hindu pilgrimage places.

PILGRIMAGE

Know Asvakranta

The temple of Asvakranta in Assam is situated in North Guwahati. An important and one of the greatest Vishnu shrines of Assam, Asvakranta is located on a rocky stratum touching the waterfront of the Brahmaputra.

Asvakranta Assam can be by motor boats that are available at Suklesvar Ghat (Guwahati). Asvakranta is favoured for its scenic beauty. From here one can enjoy the east-west expanse of Guwahati situated on the other bank of the river.

The Legend Says

Asvakranta literally means 'ascended by horses'. It is here that Sri Krishna camped with his army before he defeated and killed Narakasur.

Aswakranta is associated with Krishna-Rukamini episode. It is said that Krishna's Asva (horse) was encircled (akranta) by the enemies at this place. It is also believed by some people that the place should be caged as Asvaklanta indicating that Krishna on his way from Kundil Nagar to Dwaraka had to rest here as his horse became tired (klanta).

Sightseeing near Asvakranta

The Footprints of Lord Krishna: The rocky outcrop at the eastern side bordering the river allegedly contains a footprint, which is supposed to be that of Krishna. The devotees come to this place to perform 'Shraddha' ceremonies of the departed souls regularly.

Kurmajanardan and Anantasayi

The hillock beside the river contains two historical temples enshrining the erein images of Vishnu, known as 'Kurmajanardan' and 'Anantasayi', A long flight of steps has survived from historical times, which link the Anantasayi temple with the foothills.

Aarparuat

The Aarparuat or the flat-topped Screen-Hill is a small island, only a hundred metres off the bank of Brahmaputra River. Apart from its natural beauty, this island is the abode of thousands of white cranes, which offer added attraction to the visitors.

Know Da-Parbatia

Da-Parbatia in Tezpur Assam is the oldest and finest representation of sculptural or iconoclastic art in Assam in the form of the ruins of the door-frame of the Da-parbatia temple.

The carvings of Da-Parbatia temple displays the characteristic style of the early Gupta School of sculpture. The two legs of the door-frame have the carvings of the two Goddesses Ganga and Yamuna. Both of them are standing at the bottom with garlands in their hands. The whole frame is elaborately decorated with beautiful ornamental foliage.

Sightseeing near Da-Parbatia

Agnigarh: Agnigarh, a hillock facing the river Brahmaputra, is famous as the site of the romance of Usha and Anirudha. The Brahmaputra and a view of Tezpur can be seen from this hillock

Cole Park

An important tourist destination of Tezpur, the Cole Park has two massive stone pillars. Its beauty is enhanced by the sculptural remnants of the famous Bamuni Hills.

Bamuni Hills

Now in ruins, the Bamuni Hills still retain their charm. The sculptural remains date back to the ninth and tenth century AD.

Some Important Destinations near Da-Parbatia (Tezpur)

Tezpur, situated on the banks of the mighty Brahmaputra, is a city dipped in scenic beauty and archaeological ruins. The beauty of the city is replete with green valleys offering a view of the snow capped mountains. It was earlier known as Sonitpur. This town has numerous sights for its tourist to visit.

If you are interested in river adventure activities then Eco camp is the place for you. Located near the Jia Bhoroli river at a distance of 50 Km from Tezpur, the camp offers various adventure activities like river-rafting, fishing and angling. The camp shelters the endangered golden Mhaseer fish.

Also situated near the Jia Bhoroli river, the Nameri National Park spreads from Assam to Aruachal Pradesh. The best way to explore the Park is atop elephants. The Mithun or Indian Bison, the rare White Winged Wood Duck and other avian species can be found here.

Guwahati is just 180 km form here. You can give a visit to this commercial capital of Assam. Guwahati has numerous places of Interest for the visitors to Assam.

Hermitage of Vasistha

Know Vasisthasrama in Assam: Vasisthasrama in Assam is an important pilgrimage of Assam, situated about 10 miles to the east of the town of Guwahati. The hermitage of Vasistha

(Vasisthasrama) is situated amidst a beautiful natural surroundings. There are three streams called Sandhya, Lalita and Kanta located at this place. A bath here is said to increase longevity. A temple of Siva is also attached to the hermitage of Vasistha. This is also an ideal picnic spot for the picnickers.

The devotees visit Vasisthashrama and take bath in the stream nearby to wash off their sins. The present temple in Vasisthashrama, which is incidentally the last Ahom monument in the neighbourhood of Guwahati, was built in the second half of the 18th century by King Rajesvar Singh of the Ahom dynasty.

The Legend Says: There are many legends about sage Vasistha. There is also a legend that connects Vasistha with the origin of the Ahom kings.

It is said that, Vasistha used to do his 'sandhya' (evening prayer) in a stream near his hermitage. One day, God Indra with his queen Shachi and other heavenly women came down from heaven and began playing in the same stream. As a result of this amorous sport the water of the stream became impure. Seeing all this sage Vasistha grew furious and cursed Indra, saying that he would have sexual intercourse with a Daitya woman. Indra was at once transformed into a normal man and had sexual intercourse with a woman. He, however, granted a boon to that woman saying that the son in her womb would become a king. He was the progenitor of the Ahom dynasty.

According to some legends Vasistha was initiated into the secrets of the Sakta practices and got spiritual success. It is probable that Vasistha came down at Sandhya Kala (evening), after he was not allowed to enter the Kamakhya temple and meditated on Shiva.

9

Art, Architecture, Fair and Festivals

FINE ARTS OF ASSAM

Fine Arts of Assam has extremely rich tradition.

Sculpture and architecture

The archaic Mauryan Stupas discovered in and around Goalpara district are believed to be the earliest examples (c. 300B.C. to c. 100A.D.) of ancient art and architectural works. The monumental architectural remains discovered in Doporboteeya (Daparvatiya) archaeological site along with a beautiful doorframe in Tezpur are identified as the best examples of art works in ancient Assam with influence of Sarnath School of Art of the late Gupta period.

Gupta influence was prominent due to intense interaction of the then Kamarupa with the kingdom of Magadha. Many other sites also exhibit development of local art forms with local motifs and sometimes with similarities with those in the Southeast Asia. There are currently more than forty discovered ancient archaeological sites across Assam with numerous sculptural and architectural remains. Moreover, there are examples of several Late-Middle Age art and architectural works including hundreds of sculptures and motifs along with many remaining temples, palaces and other buildings. The motifs available on the walls of the buildings such as Rang Ghar, Joydoul, etc. are remarkable examples of art works.

Paintings

Painting is an ancient tradition of Assam. The ancient practices can be known from the accounts of the Chinese traveller Xuanzang (7th century CE). The account mentions that Bhaskaravarma, the king of Kamarupa has gifted several items to Harshavardhana, the king of Magadha including paintings and painted objects, some of which were on Assamese silk. Many of the manuscripts available from the Middle Ages bear excellent examples of traditional paintings. The most famous of such medieval works are available in the Hastividyarnava (A Treatise on Elephants), the Chitra Bhagawata and in the Gita Govinda. The medieval painters used locally manufactured painting materials such as the colours of hangool and haital. The medieval Assamese literature also refers to chitrakars and patuas. Traditional Assamese paintings have been influenced by the motifs and designs in the medieval works such as the Chitra Bhagawata.

There are several renowned contemporary painters in Assam. The Guwahati Art College in Guwahati is one of the government institution for tertiary education. The Department of Visual Arts Assam University (Central University)is one of the only department of North East India which along with the specialization programme in Applied Arts, Graphics,and Paintings have PhD programme in Visual Arts. Moreover, there are several art-societies and non-government initiatives across the state and the Gauhati Artists' Guild is a front-runner organisation based in Guwahati.

FAIRS AND FESTIVALS IN ASSAM

The fairs and festivals in Assam are a fine reflection of the state's jest for life. Indeed, the people of Assam are a merry lot who lose no opportunity to celebrate. So it is not surprising to see the state's festival calendar choc a bloc with a variety of fairs and festivals that attract visitors from all over.

Right from yearly fairs like the Ambubachi Mela to the Rangali Bihu festival, there are many fairs and festivals in Assam to speak of. The fact that Assam is a melting pot for varied races and cultures adds more to its appeal. So its needless to mention that the Assam fairs and festivals have their roots in a varied number of faiths and beliefs.

For centuries, the people of Assam have been celebrating all fairs and festivals with equal enthusiasm and fervor. The spirit of togetherness is so well reflected by the fairs and festivals of Assam that one is often left mesmerized. So if you time your visit well, you can surely be a part of some of the most popular fairs and festivals celebrated in Assam.

Apart from regional festivals, the people of Assam also celebrate all the national festivals of India. From the lights of Diwali to the patriotic colors of the Independence Day, you can see them all in Assam, India. So the next time you travel to Assam, time your visit in a way that you are able to be a part of some of its most colorful festivals.

10

Education

INTRODUCTION

Assam schools are run by the Indian government, government of Assam or by private organisations. Medium of instruction is mainly in Assamese, English or Bengali. Most of the schools follow the state's examination board which is called the Secondary Education Board of Assam. Almost all private schools follow the Central Board for Secondary Education (CBSE), Indian Certificate of Secondary Education(ICSE) and Indian School Certificate (ISC) syllabuses.

Assamese language is the main medium in educational institutions but Bengali language is also taught as a major Indian language. In Guwahati and Digboi, many Jr. basic School and Jr. high School are Nepali linguistic and all the teachers are British Gorkha. Nepali is included by Assam State Secondary Board, Assam Higher Secondary Education Council and Gauhati University in their HSLC, higher secondary and graduation level respectively. In some junior basic and higher secondary schools and colleges, Nepali language speaking British Gorkha teachers and lecturers are appointed.

The capital, Dispur, contains institutions of higher education for students of the north-eastern region. Cotton College, Guwahati, dates back to the 19th century. Assam has several institutions for tertiary education and research.

Universities, Colleges and Institutions include:

Universities

- Assam University
- Assam Agricultural University, Jorhat
- Assam Don Bosco University, (private)
- Assam down town University, (private)
- Assam Rajiv Gandhi University of Cooperative Management, (ARGUCOM), Sivasagar
- Assam Science and Technology University, Guwahati
- Assam Women's University, Jorhat
- Bodoland University, Kokrajhar
- Cotton University
- Dibrugarh University, Dibrugarh
- Gauhati University, Guwahati
- Kaziranga University, Jorhat (private)
- Krishnaguru Adhyatmik Vishvavidyalaya
- Krishna Kanta Handique State Open University
- Kumar Bhaskar Varma Sanskrit and Ancient Studies University
- Mahapurusha Srimanta Sankaradeva Viswavidyalaya
- National Law University and Judicial Academy, Assam
- Royal Global University (private)
- Srimanta Sankaradeva University of Health Sciences
- Tezpur University,Tezpur

Medical colleges

- Assam Medical College in Dibrugarh
- Fakhruddin Ali Ahmed Medical College, Barpeta
- Gauhati Medical College and Hospital in Guwahati
- Jorhat Medical College and Hospital, Jorhat
- Regional Dental College, Guwahati
- Silchar Medical College and Hospital, Silchar
- Tezpur Medical College & Hospital, Tezpur

Engineering and technological colleges

- Indian Institute of Information Technology, Guwahati
- National Institute of Technology, Silchar,
- Assam Engineering College in Guwahati,
- Assam Science and Technology University
- Bineswar Brahma Engineering College, Kokrajhar
- Central Institute of Technology, Kokrajhar,
- Girijananda Chowdhury Institute of Management and Technology, Guwahati
- Girijananda Chowdhury Institute of Management and Technology, Tezpur
- Indian Institute of Technology in Guwahati,
- Institute of Engineering and Technology, Dibrugarh University
- Institute of Science and Technology, Guwahati University
- Jorhat Institute of Science & Technology, Jorhat
- Jorhat Engineering College in Jorhat.
- NETES Institute of Technology & Science Mirza,
- Barak Valley Engineering College Nirala Karimganj
- Golaghat Engineering College Golaghat

Research institutes present in the state include National Research Centre on Pig, (ICAR) in Guwahati.

HISTORY OF ELEMENTARY EDUCATION

The name of the organization in Directorate of Elementary Education under department of Education, Govt. of Assam. It is located at Kahilipara, Guwahati 781019, Assam.

The Director of the Elementary Education, Assam is the head of the Directorate of the Elementary Education.

The Organizational structure pattern of the staff of this Directorate stated diagrammatically as in the Table.

The Directorate of Elementary Education, Assam was established as a separate establishment in July, 1977, with its

Head quarter at Kahilipara, Guwahati—19, for management of Elementary Education to achieve the following objectives.

1. To decentralize management at schools up to Block level, and
2. To organize activities towards attainment of universalization of Elementary Education (UEE).

Earlier this Directorate was belong to erstwhile Directorate of Public Instruction (DPI) functioning independently for Assam in 1947.

This Directorate is responsible for administration control, development and expansion, inspection, supervision, monitoring and evaluation of Elementary Education in Assam.

The services of all Sub-divisional Education Officers (Deputy Inspector of Schools) and other subordinate inspecting officers (Sub-Inspector and Assistant Sub-Inspector of Schools) all over the state have been placed under this Directorate.

All Junior Basic Training Centre (22 Nos.), which train-up the Primary School Teachers and all Normal Training Schools (7 Nos.) which train-up the Middle School Teachers have also been brought under the Directorate, including the Basic Training College at Titabor, which also train-up Middle School teachers.

The Elementary stage of education in Assam covers classes from Class I to Class VII and covers students for the age group of 6 - 14 years.

BOARD OF SECONDARY EDUCATION, ASSAM

Board of Secondary Education, Assam, or SEBA as it is also known, is the state level authority for conducting examinations and providing assurance for the quality of education imparted in schools within Assam that are affiliated to it.

High School Leaving Certificate (HSLC) is the award given through the authority of this board to students who have passed the HSLC examination successfully.

It was established in 1962.

ASSAM AGRICULTURAL UNIVERSITY

Assam Agricultural University was established in 1969 under the Assam Agricultural University Act 1968 (Assam Act XXIV of1968) vide Governor's notification LJL 18/67/10 dated the January 2, 1969.

The objectives of the University are:

- To make provision for imparting education to the people in agriculture and other allied branches of learning
- To further the advancement of learning and research in agriculture and other allied sciences
- To undertake the extension of such sciences especially to the rural people of the state.

Colleges under Assam Agricultural University against various faculties are:

A. Faculty of Agriculture

* College of Agriculture, Jorhat
* Biswanath College of Agriculture, Biswanath Chariali

B. Faculty of Veterinary Science

* College of Veterinary Science, Khanapara
* Lakhimpur College of Veterinary Science, Azad

C. Faculty of Home Science

* College of Home Science, Jorhat

D. Faculty of Fisheries Science

* College of Fisheries Science, Raha

EDUCATION IN ASSAM

Assam is a state in northeastern India. In 2011, the literacy rate of Assam was estimated to be 73.18% (78.81% male and 67.27% female).The literacy rate of Assam is slightly below the national average of 74.04%.

General

School education in Assam is imparted through a number of pre-primary, primary, middle, high and higher secondary schools. The Government of Assam has implemented free and compulsory education for students up to the age of 14. Schools in Assam are either state run or under the management of private organizations. The syllabus at primary schools is established by the Directorate of Elementary Education, Assam. While most schools are affiliated to SEBA, there are several schools in the state affiliated to the Central Board of Secondary Education (CBSE) or North East National Board of School Education (NENBSE).

Medium of instruction

The language used for instruction is usually Assamese. there are a number of schools in that also use English. English is used to teach at almost all higher educational institutions. Many State Government affiliated and all the CBSE affiliated schools in the state use English as their medium of instruction at the Higher Secondary level.

LIST OF COLLEGES AFFILIATED TO GAUHATI UNIVERSITY

B.ED colleges

- Anunduram Baruah Academy B.Ed. College, Pathsala (Barpeta)
- Ataur Rahman College of Education, Udmari Kalgachi (Barpeta)
- Dr. Anita Baruah Sarmah College of Education, Guwahati (Kamrup)
- Dakshin Guwahati B.Ed. College, Guwahati
- Damdama B.Ed. College, Kulhati (Kamrup)
- Deomornoi B.Ed. College, Deomornoi (Darrang)
- Dudhnoi Teachers Training College, Dudhnoi (Goalpara)
- East Gauhati B.Ed. College, Guwahati

- Faculty College of Education, North Gauhati (Kamrup)
- Gossaigaon B.Ed. College, Gossaigaon (Kokrajhar)
- Govt. Banikanta College of Teacher Education, Guwahati (Kamrup)
- Govt. College of Teacher's Education, Kokrajhar (Kokrajhar)
- Govt. College of Teacher's Education (CTE), Tezpur (Sonitpur)
- Gurudev Kalicharan Brahma College,Tipkai (Kokrajhar)
- Imperial College of Education, Dispur (Kamrup)
- K.R.D. College of Education, Chhaygaon (Kamrup)
- Kaliabor College of Education, Kuwaritol (Nagaon)
- Krishna Bora B.Ed. College, Lanka ASSAM
- Mangaldai Govt. Teachers' Training College, Mangaldai (Darrang)
- Nalbari B.Ed. College, Nalbari
- National Institute for Teacher Education, Khetri (Kamrup) Assam
- P.G. College of Education, Tezpur (Sonitpur)
- Pachim Nalbari B.Ed. College, Nalbari (Nalbari)
- Pragjyotish B.Ed. College, Pacharia
- Rangia Teacher Training College, Rangia (Kamrup)
- Sipajhar B.Ed. College, Sipajhar (Darrang
- West Guwahati College of Education, kotihati

Law colleges

- Barpeta Law College Barpeta
- Biswanath Law College Sonitpur
- Bongaigaon Law College Bongaigaon
- BRM Govt. Law College KAmrup
- Dr. B. R. Ambedkar Law College Kamrup
- Dhubri Law College
- Dispur Law College

- Goalpara Law College
- Govt. B.R. Medhi Law College, Guwahati
- J.B. Law College Kamrup
- Kokrajhar Law College
- Mangaldai Law College, DArrang
- Morigaon Law College
- Nalbari Law College
- NEF Law College
- Nowgong Law College
- Tezpur Law College
- University Law College, GU

List of other colleges in alphabetical order

Cotton College, Guwahati

- A.D.P. College, Nagaon (Nagaon)
- Abhayapuri College, Abhayapuri (Bongaigaon)
- Agia College, Agia (Goalpara)
- Alamganj Rangamati College, Alamganj (Dhubri)
- Alhaz Sunai Bibi Choudhury College, Lanka (Nagaon)
- Amrit Chandra Thakuria Commerce College (Kamrup)
- Anandaram Dhekial Phookan College, Nagaon
- Anunduram Baruah Academy B.Ed. College, Pathsala (Barpeta)

- Arya Vidyapeeth College, Guwahati
- Asian Institute of Nursing Education, G.N.R.C. Campus, Dispur
- Asom Sikshak Prasikshan Mahavidyalaya, Guwahati
- Ataur Rahman College of Education, Udmari Kalgachi (Barpeta)
- B.H.B. College, Sarupeta (Barpeta)
- Bagadhar Brahma Kishan College, Jalahghat (Baksa)
- Bimala Prasad Chaliha College, Nagarbera (Kamrup)
- B. Borooah College, Guwahati (Kamrup)
- Baihata Chariali B.Ed. College, Baihata Chariali (Kamrup)
- Bajali College, Pathsala (Barpeta)
- Bajali T.T. College, Patacharkuchi, Barpeta (Barpeta)
- Bamundi Mahavidyalaya, Bamundi (Kamrup)
- Baosi Banikanta Kakoti College, Nagaon (Barpeta)
- Bapujee College, Sarthebari (Barpeta)
- Barama College, Barama (Baksa)
- Barbhag College, Kalag (Nalbari)
- Barkhetri College, Mukalmua (Nalbari)
- Barnagar B.Ed. College, Sorbhog (Barpeta)
- Barnagar College, Sorbhog (Barpeta)
- Barpeta B.T. College, Barpeta
- Barpeta Bongaigaon College, Langla (Barpeta)
- Barpeta College, Barpeta
- Barpeta Girls' College, Barpeta
- Barpeta Road Howli College, Howli (Barpeta)
- Baska College, Baganpara (Baksa)
- Basugaon College, Basugaon (Kokrajhar)
- Batadraba Sri Sri Sankardev College, Batadraba (Nagaon)
- Behali Degree College, Borgang (Sonitpur)
- Beltola College, Guwahati

- Bengtol College, Bengtol (Kokrajhar)
- Bezara Anchalik College, Bezara (Kamrup)
- Bhawanipur Anchalik College, Bhawanipur (Barpeta)
- Bholanath College, Dhubri
- Bhuragaon College, Bhuragaon (Morigaon)
- Bijni College, Bijni (Bongaigaon)
- Bikali College, Dhupdhara (Goalpara)
- Bilasipara College, Bilasipara (Dhubri)
- Binandi Chandra Medhi College, Ramdia (Kamrup)
- Birjhora Kanya Mahavidyalaya, Bongaigaon (Bongaigaon)
- Birjhora Mahavidyalaya, Bongaigaon (Bongaigaon)
- Biswanath College, Chariali (Sonitpur)
- Biswanath College of Education, Chariali (Sonitpur)
- Biswanath Commerce College, Biswanath (Sonitpur)
- BMBB Commerce College, Guwahati
- Bodofa U.N. Brahma College, Dotma (Kokrajhar)
- Bongaigaon B.Ed. College, Bongaigaon
- Bongaigaon College, Bongaigaon
- Bajali Teacher's Training College, Pattacharkuchi, Barpeta.
- Chaiduar College, Gohpur (Sonitpur)
- Chhamaria Anchalik College, Chhamaria (Kamrup)
- Chandrapur College, Chandrapur (Kamrup)
- Charaibahi College, Charaibahi (Morigaon)
- Chariduar College, Gohpur (Sonitpur)
- Chatia College, Sootia (Sonitpur)
- Chhaygaon College, Chhaygaon (Kamrup)
- Chilarai College, Golakganj (Dhubri)
- Chunari College (chunari)
- College of Education, Boko (Kamrup)
- College of Education, Guwahati (Kamrup)
- College of Education, Morigaon
- College of Education, Nagaon

- Commerce College, Kokrajhar (Kokrajhar)
- Dr. Anita Baruah Sarmah College of Education, Guwahati (Kamrup)
- Dr. B. Borooah Cancer Institute
- Dr. B. K. B. College, Puranigudam (Nagaon)
- Dr. Birinchi Kumar Barooah College, Puranigudam (Nagaon)
- Dakshin Guwahati B.Ed. College, Guwahati
- Dakshin Kamrup College, Mirza (Kamrup)
- Dakshin Kamrup Girls' College, Mirza (Kamrup)
- Dakshin Nalbari Mahavidyalaya, Niz-Bahjani (Nalbari)
- Dakshinpat College, Bhomoraguri (Nagaon)
- Dalgoma Anchalik College, Matia (Goalpara)
- Damdama B.Ed. College, Kulhati (Kamrup)
- Damdama College, Kulhati (Kamrup)
- Darrang College, Tezpur (Sonitpur)
- Deomornoi B.Ed. College, Deomornoi (Darrang)
- Deomornoi Degree College, Deomornoi (Darrang)
- Dhamdhama Anchalik College, Dhamdhama (Nalbari)
- Dharamtul College, Ahatguri (Morigaon))
- Dharmasala College, Dharmasala (Dhubri)
- Dhing College, Dhing (Nagaon)
- Dhubri P.G.T.T. College, Jhagrarpar (Dhubri)
- Dhubri Girls' College, Dhubri
- Dimoria College, Khetri (Kamrup)
- Dispur College, Guwahati (Kamrup)
- Dronacharjya College, Barpeta Road (Barpeta)
- Dudhnoi College, Dudhnoi (Goalpara)
- Dudhnoi Teachers Training College, Dudhnoi (Goalpara)
- Duni Degree College (Darrang)
- East Gauhati B.Ed. College, Guwahati (Kamrup)
- F.A. Ahmed College, Goraimari, Tukrapara (Kamrup)

- Faculty College of Education, North Gauhati (Kamrup)
- Fakiragram College, Fakiragram (Kokrajhar)
- G.L. Choudhury College, Barpeta Road (Barpeta)
- Gauhati Commerce College, Guwahati (Kamrup)
- Ghanakanta Baruah College, Morigaon (Morigaon)
- Girls' College Kokrajhar, Kokrajhar (Kokrajhar)
- Goalpara College, Goalpara (Goalpara)
- Golden College (RATHNAPITH)
- Goreswar College, Goreswar (Baksa)
- Gossaigaon B.Ed. College, Gossaigaon (Kokrajhar)
- Gossaigaon College, Gossaigaon (Kokrajhar)
- Govt. B.T. College, Goalpara
- Govt. K.K. Handique Sanskrit College, Guwahati (Kamrup)
- Govt. Banikanta College of Teacher Education, Guwahati (Kamrup)
- Govt. College of Teacher's Education, Kokrajhar (Kokrajhar)
- Govt. College of Teacher's Education (CTE), Tezpur (Sonitpur)
- Govt. Shikshan Mahavidyalaya, Nagaon (Nagaon)
- Guwahati College, Guwahati (Kamrup)
- Gyanpeeth Degree College, Nikashi (Baksa)
- Habraghat Mahavidyalaya, Krishnai (Goalpara)
- Haji Ajmal Ali College (Nagaon)
- Haji Anfor Ali College, Doboka (Nagaon)
- Halakura College, Mahamayahat (Dhubri)
- Hamidabad College, Jamadarhat (Dhubri)
- Handique Girls College, Azara, Guwahati
- Harendra Citra College, Naligaon (Barpeta)
- Hari Gayatri Das College, Guwahati (Kamrup)
- Hatichong College, Hatichong (Nagaon)
- Hatidhura College, Hatidhura (Kokrajhar)

- Hatsingimari College, Hatsingimari (Dhubri)
- Hindustan College, Guwahati
- Hojai College, Hojai (Nagaon)
- Hojai Girls' College, Hojai (Nagaon)
- Icon Commerce College, Guwahati (Kamrup)
- Imperia College of Education, Dispur (Kamrup)
- Indira Gandhi College, Boitamari (Bongaigaon)
- Institute of Strategic Business Management (ISBM), Guwahati (Kamrup)
- Jagiroad College, Jagiroad (Morigaon)
- Jaleswar College, Tapoban (Goalpara)
- Jamduar College, Saraibil (Kokrajhar)
- Jamunamukh College, Jamunamukh (Nagaon)
- Janapriya College, Garemari (Barpeta)
- Janata College, (Serfanguri), Kokrajhar
- Jawaharlal Nehru College, Boko (Kamrup)
- Juria College, Fakuli Pathar (Nagaon)
- K.C. Das Commerce College, Guwahati (Kamrup)
- K.R.B. Girls' College, Guwahati
- K.R.D. College of Education, Chhaygaon (Kamrup)
- Kalabari College, Kalabari (Sonitpur)
- Kalaguru Bishnu Rabha Degree College, Orang (Udalguri)
- Kaliabor College, Kuwaritol (Nagaon)
- Kaliabor College of Education, Kuwaritol (Nagaon)
- Kamrup College, Chamata (Nalbari)
- Kampur College, Kampur (Nagaon)
- Kanpai Bordoloi College, Borchila (Morigaon)
- Kanya Mahavidyalaya, Guwahati
- Karmashree Hiteswar Saikia College, Guwahati
- Katahguri College, Tuktuki (Nagaon)
- Kayakuchi College, Kayakuchi (Barpeta)
- Khagarijan College, Chotahaibar (Nagaon)

- Kharupetia College, Kharupetia (Darrang)
- Khetri Dharmapur College, Bari (Nalbari)
- Khoirabari College, Khoirabari (Udalguri)
- Kokrajhar Government College, Kokrajhar (Kokrajhar)
- Kokrajhar Music and Fine Arts College, Kokrajhar
- Krishna Bora B.Ed. College, Lanka
- Krishanaguru Mahavidyalaya, Nasatra (Barpeta)
- L.C. Bharali College, Guwahati
- L.G.B. Girls' College, Tezpur (Sonitpur)
- Lokopriya Gopinath Bordoloi Regional Institute of Mental Health
- Lachit Barphookan Commerce Academy, Morikalong (Nagaon)
- Lakhipur College, Lakhipur (Goalpara)
- Lalit Chandra Bharali College, Guwahati
- Lanka Mahavidyalaya, Lanka (Nagaon)
- Lokanayak Omeo Kumar Das College, Dhekiajuli (Sonitpur)
- Luitparia College, Kalairdia (Barpeta)
- Lumding College, Lumding (Nagaon)
- M.C. College, Barpeta (Barpeta)
- M.N.C. Balika Mahavidyalaya, Nalbari
- Madhab Choudhury College, Barpeta
- Madhya Kamrup College, Subha, Chenga (Barpeta)
- Madhya Kampeeth College, Borka, Pub-Borka (Kamrup)
- Manabendra Sarma Girls' College, Rangia (Kamrup)
- Mancachar College, Mancachar (Dhubri)
- Mandia Anchalik College, Mandia (Barpeta)
- Mangaldai Govt. Teachers' Training College, Mangaldai (Darrang)
- Mangaldai College, Mangaldai (Darrang)
- Mangaldai Commerce College, Mangaldai (Darrang)

- Mangaldai Degree Girls College, Magnaldai (Darrang)
- Mahatma Gandhi College, Chalantapara (Bongaigaon)
- Majbat College, Majbat (Udalguri)
- Manikpur Anchalik College, Manikpur (Bongaigaon)
- Mayang Anchalik College, Raja-Mayang (Morigaon)
- Mazbat College, Mazbat (Darrang)
- Milanjyoti College, Itervita (Barpeta)
- Missamari College, Missamari (Sonitpur)
- Moirabari College, Moirabari (Morigaon)
- Morigaon College, Morigaon (Morigaon)
- Murazar College, Murazar (Nagaon)
- Mushalpur College, Mushalpur, (Baksa)
- Nagaon G. N. D. G. Commerce College, Panigaon (Nagaon)
- Nabajyoti College, Kalgachia (Barpeta)
- Nalbari B.Ed. College, Nalbari
- Nalbari College, Nalbari
- Nalbari Commerce College, Nalbari
- Nalbari Sanskrit College, Nalbari (Nalbari)
- Narangi Anchalik Mahavidyalaya, Guwahati (Kamrup)
- National Institute for Teacher Education, Khetri (Kamrup)
- Navasakti College, Majgoan (Barpeta)
- Nirmal Haloi College, Patacharkuchi (Barpeta)
- Nonoi College, Nonoi (Nagaon)
- North Gauhati College, Guwahati
- North Kamrup College, Baghmara (Barpeta)
- Nowgong College, Nagaon
- Nowgong Girls' College, Nagaon
- P.G. College of Education, Tezpur (Sonitpur)
- Pandu College, maligaon
- Paschim Guwahati Mahavidyalaya, Guwahati
- Paschim Barigog Anchalik Mahavidyalaya, Baranghati (Kamrup)

- Pachim Nalbari B.Ed. College, Nalbari (Nalbari)
- Patidarrang College, Loch (Kamrup)
- Pragjyotish B.Ed. College, Pacharia
- Pragjyotish College, Guwahati
- Pramathesh Barua College, Gauripur (Dhubri)
- Province College, Ganeshguri
- Progati College, Agomani (Dhubri)
- Pub-Bongsor College, Pacharia
- Pub Kamrup College, Baihata Chariali (Kamrup)
- Puthimari College, Soneswar (Kamrup)
- Pune Institute Of Business Management, Guwahati campus (Kamrup)
- R.C. Saharia T.T. College, Tangla (Udalguri)
- Radha Govinda Baruah College, Guwahati
- Raha College, Ranha (Nagaon)
- Rajiv Gandhi Memorial College, Lengtisinga (Bongaigaon)
- Rampur Anchalik College, Rampur (Kamrup)
- Rangapara College, Rangapara (Sonitpur)
- Rangia College, Rangia (Kamrup)
- Rangia Teacher Training College, Rangia (Kamrup)
- Ratnapith College, Chapar (Dhubri)
- Rupahi College, Rupahi (Nagaon)
- Salbari College, Salbari (Baksa)
- Samaguri College, Samaguri (Nagaon)
- Sapatgram College, Sapatgram (Dhubri)
- Saraighat College, Changsari (Kamrup)
- Science College, Kokrajhar (Kokrajhar)
- Sikshan Mahavidyalaya, Nagaon
- Sipajhar B.Ed. College, Sipajhar (Darrang)
- Sipajhar College, Sipajhar (Darrang)
- Sonapur College, Sonapur (Kamrup)
- Sontali Anchalik College, Mahatoli (Kamrup)

- South Salmara College, South Salmara (Dhubri)
- Srimanta Sankar Madhab Mahavidyalay, Bhatkuchi (Barpeta)
- State College of Music, Guwahati
- Sualkuchi Budram Madhab Satradhikar College, Sualkuchi (Kamrup)
- Suren Das College, Hajo (Kamrup)
- Swami Yogananda Giri College, Saktiashram (Kokrajhar)
- Swadeshi College of Commerce, Guwahati
- SDP College of Teacher Education,Tihu
- T.H.B. College, Jamugurihat (Sonitpur)
- Tamulpur College, Tamulpur (Baksa)
- Tamulpur Degree College, Tamulpur (Baksa)
- Tangla College, Tangla (Udalguri)
- Teachers' Training College, Mirza (Kamrup)
- Tezpur College, Tezpur (Sonitpur)
- Thamna Anchalik Degree College, Thamna (Baksa)
- Tihu College, Tihu (Nalbari)
- U.N. Brahma College, Kajalgaon, (Chirang)
- Udalguri College, Udalguri (Udalguri)
- Udali College, Bamungaon (Nagaon)
- Uttar Barpeta College, Sankuchi (Barpeta)
- Uttar Kampith Mahavidyalaya, Jagara (Nalbari)
- Vidya Bharati College, Kendua (Kamrup)
- West Gauhati Commerce College, Guwahati (Maligaon)
- West Goalpara College, barbhita (Goalpara)
- West Guwahati College of Education, kotihati

ASSAM UNIVERSITY

Assam University is a teaching-cum-affiliating Central University. The university has sixteen schools which offer Social Sciences, Humanities, Languages, Life Sciences, Physical Sciences, Environmental Sciences, Information Sciences, Technology and Management Studies. There are 42 departments under these sixteen schools. The five districts under the jurisdiction of Assam University have 56 undergraduate colleges. Assam University is an institutional signatory to the Global Universities Network for Innovation (GUNI), Barcelona and United Nations Global Compact (UNGC) for its commitment to educational social responsibilities.

The main campus, in an area of 600 acres (2.4 km), is located at Durgakona, near Irongmara about 20 km from Silchar, while a second campus of the university is at Diphu, in the East Karbi Anglong district of Assam.

History

The history of Assam University is the history of people's struggle in Barak Valley. The "Saheed Minar" situated near the entrance of the university commemorates the history of Bengali language movement of this valley.

Schools and departments

The major teaching schools of the university along with the departments under them are:

- Abanindranath Tagore School of Creative Arts and Communication Studies
- Department of Mass Communication
- Department of Visual Arts
- Albert Einstein School of Physical Science
- Department of Mathematics
- Department of Chemistry
- Department of Physics
- Department of Statistics
- Department of Computer Science
- Aryabhatta School of Earth Sciences
- Department of Earth Sciences
- Ashutosh Mukhopadhyay School of Education
- Department of Educational Science

- Deshabandhu Chittaranjan School of Legal Studies
- Department of Law
- E. P. Odam School of Environmental Sciences
- Department of Ecology and Environmental Science
- Hargobind Khurana School of Life Sciences
- Department of Life Science & Bioinformatics
- Department of Biotechnology
- Department of Microbiology
- Jadunath Sarkar School of Social Sciences
- Department of Anthropology
- Department of History
- Department of Political Science
- Department of Social Work
- Department of Sociology
- Jawaharlal Nehru School of Management Studies
- Department of Business Administration
- Mahatma Gandhi School of Economics and Commerce
- Department of Economics
- Department of Commerce
- Rabindranath Tagore School of Indian Languages and Cultural Studies
- Department of Assamese
- Department of Bengali
- Department of Hindi
- Department of Indian Comparative Literature
- Department of Linguistics
- Department of Manipuri
- Department of Sanskrit
- Sarvepalli Radhakrishnan School of Philosophy
- Department of Philosophy
- Shushrutu School of Medical and Paramedical Sciences
- Department of Pharmaceutical Sciences

- Suniti Kumar Chattopadhyay School of English and Foreign Language Studies
- Department of English
- Department of Arabic
- Department of French
- Department of Linguistics
- Department of Comparative Studies
- Department of Urdu
- Swami Vivekananda School of Library Sciences
- Department of Library & Information Science
- Triguna Sen School of Technology
- Department of Agricultural Engineering
- Department of Electronics & Communication Engineering
- Department of Computer Science & Engineering
- Department of Applied Science & Humanities

Ranking

Assam University was ranked 87 among universities by the National Institutional Ranking Framework (NIRF) of 2018 and in the 101-150 band overall.

Affiliated colleges

All the colleges in the 5 districts of South Assam, viz, Cachar, Karimganj, Hailakandi, North Cachar Hills or Dima Hasao and Karbi Anglong district fall within university's jurisdiction. Till the year 2013 there were 50 colleges which include Degree colleges, a Medical college, a few Law colleges and Teachers' Training colleges. Notable affiliated colleges include:

- Srikishan Sarda College. Hailakandi
- Janata College.Kabuganj
- Cachar College, Silchar
- Diphu Government College, Diphu
- Karimganj College, Karimganj

- Gurucharan College, Silchar
- Silchar Medical College and Hospital till 2009
- Women's College, Silchar

TEZPUR UNIVERSITY

Tezpur University was established as an Indian Central University located in Tezpur in the state of Assam, India.

History

Tezpur University was established in 1994, by an Act of Parliament (Act. No. 45, 1: Foundation of Tezpur University, 1993) in 1994. Tezpur University is a unitary type university. The former Prime Minister of India, Sri P V Narasimha Rao declared the opening of the University.

The objectives of Central University are: it shall strive to offer employment oriented and inter-disciplinary courses, mostly, at postgraduate level to meet local, regional aspirations and development needs of the State of Assam; offer courses and promote research in areas which are of special relevance to the region and in emerging areas in science and technology; promote national integration and study of rich cultural heritage of the region and, in particular, the diverse ethnic, linguistic and tribal cultures of the State; utilize "distance education techniques" to provide access to higher education for large segments of the population, the disadvantaged groups living in remote and rural areas; to upgrade the professional knowledge and skills of in service personnel for life-long learning.

Campus

The University campus is at Napaam about 15 km. East of Tezpur, the head quarter of Sonitpur District of Assam. Napaam is a rural area surrounded by peace loving people of diverse caste, religion and language; yet it presents the unique feature of unity in diversity. The Napaam campus of the University is in a plot of an area of 242 acres (0.98 km^2) of land. The campus is bounded by pucca walls. Napaam is linked by a PWD road from the National Highway No. 37A at almost midpoint between Kalia-Bhomora bridge and Misson Chariali. Tezpur is linked by road and rail with the rest of the state and the country.

There is also a tri-weekly flight service between Kolkata and Tezpur. The institute is situated in a scenic place called *Napaam* surrounded by greenery and with many historic as well as tourist places nearby, including Ganesh Ghat, Agnigarh etc.

Education

Tezpur University is the first university in India to offer the course Master of Technology in *Computational Seismology* and also one of the few universities in India to have its own *Department of Energy*. The Department of Electronics at Tezpur University is the first of its kind in India to introduce an interdisciplinary Master of Technology program in Bioelectronics. The first class graduated in June 2006. The university offers various undergraduate, postgraduate and doctoral programs in following academic divisions:

- School of Science & Technology
- School of Humanities & Social Science
- School of Energy, Environmental & Natural Resources
- School of Management Science
- School of Engineering

School of Science & Technology

This school provides education as well as various diploma, undergraduate, postgraduate, and research programmes related to natural sciences in following subjects:

- Department of Physics
- Department of Chemical Sciences
- Department of Mathematical Sciences
- Department of Molecular Biology and Biotechnology
- Department of Food Processing Technology

School of Humanities & Social Science

This school provides education as well as various diploma, undergraduate, postgraduate, and research programmes related to arts and social sciences in following Departments:

- Department of English and Foreign Languages
- Department of Cultural Studies
- Department of Mass Communication and Journalism
- Department of Sociology

School of Energy, Environmental & Natural Resources

This school provides education as well as various diploma, undergraduate, postgraduate, and research programmes related to Energy Conservation and reuse in following Departments:

Department of Energy

Initially a centre for Non-conventional Energy was established in the university in 1995, in which offered a One-year Diploma Programme in Non-conventional Energy Technology. The centre was then converted to Department of Energy in 1996, with an aim to produce a manpower pool in the field of Energy at different levels, develop new and efficient energy technologies and carryout research & development work and extension activities in diverse areas of energy. The thrust areas of research are Biomass energy, Biofuels, Solar energy, Wind energy, Hydroenergy and Energy conservation and Management. At present it is a "DST-FIST Sponsored Department". The Department is now offering M.Tech. in Energy Technology for engineering graduates and master degree holders in Physics and Chemistry and Ph.D. in Energy Related areas for the Master degree holder in Science & Engineering/ Technology.

Bibliography

Agarwal, S.K. : *Incidence of Anestrus in Buffaloes,* M.V.Sc. Thesis Submitted to RohilKhand University, Bareilly, 1989.

Bordoloi, B.N. : *Chomangkan (The death ceremony performed by the Krbis)*, Guwahati, Tribal Research Institute, Assam, 1982.

Boro, Anil : *Folk Literature of the Bodos : An Introduction*, Adhunik Prakashan, Guwahati, 2001.

Burges, A. &. Raw, F. : *Soil Biology,* Academic Press, London, 1967.

Champion, H.G. and Seth, S.K. : *A Revised Survey of the Forest Types of India*, Publication Division, Delhi, 1968.

Das, Rajat Kanti : *Manipur Tribal Scene*, Inter-India Publications, Delhi, 1985.

Dawar, Jagadish Lal : *Cultural Identity of Tribes of North East India*, Commonwealth Publishers, New Delhi, 2003.

Deuri, R.K. : *The Sulung*, Research Department, Govt of Arunachal Pradesh, Shillong, 1982.

Devi, Premlata : *Socio and Religious Institution of the Bodos*, Geophil publishing House, Guwahati, 1998.

Gupta, A K : *Status and Conservation of Non-human Primate in Tripura*, University of Louis Pasteur, Strasbourg, 1994.

Hodson, T.C. : *The Meitheis*, B.R. Publishing Corp., Delhi, 1908.

Lal, R.B. and Ramakantha, V. : *A Status Report on the Tropical Forests of Manipur*, Indian Environmental Society, Delhi, 1991.

Macfadyen, A. : *Animal Ecology: Aims and Methods,* Pitman, London, 1957.

Meerwarth, A.M. : *The Andamese, Nicobarese, and Hill Tribes of Assam*, Spectrum Publications, Gauhati, 1919.

Mittermeier, R. A.; Myers, N. and Mittermeier, C. G. : *Hotspots, Earth's Biologically Richest and Most Endangered Terrestrial Ecoregions,* Cemex Conservation International, Cemex, Sierra Madre, Mexico City, 2000.

Nath, R.M. : *The Background of Assamese Culture*, Dutta Baruah and Co., Gauhati, 1948.

Nautiyal, S. : *Ecosystem Function of Buffer Zone Villages of Nanda Devi Biosphere Reserve*, H.N.B. Garhwal University, Srinagar (Garhwal), India, 1998.

Pegul, Nomal : *The Mishings*. Published by Mrs. Monumati Pegu, Dhemaji (Assam), 1981.

Sarkar, S. : *Taxonomy of Oribatid Mites from the Soils of Tripura*, Oxford & IBH Publishing Co. Pvt. Ltd., New Delhi, 1991.

Saxena, N.C. : *Towards Sustainable Forestry in U.P. Hills*, Lal Bahadur Shastri National Academy of Administration, Mussoorie, U.P., 1995.

Singh, J.S. and Yadava, P.S. : *Seasonal Variation in Composition, Plant Biomass and Net Primary Productivity of a Tropical Grassland at Kurukshetra*, India, 1974.

Singh, Ram Gopal : *The Kukis of Tripura*, Directorate of Research, Government of Tripura, 1981.

Singh,Y. P.; Gangwar, S. K.; Kumar, D. : *Rodent Pests and Their Management in North Eastern Hill Region*, ICAR Research Complex for NEH Region, Meghalaya, 1995.

Soppitt, C. A. : *The Kuki-Lushai Tribes*, Tribal Research Institute, Aizawl, 1893.

Srivastava : *Among the Wanchos*. Government of Arunachal Pradesh, Shillong, 1970.

Thanga, Lal Biak : *The Mizos*. United Publishers, Gauhati, 1978.

Tiwari, J.C. and Singh, S.P. : *Vegetation Analysis of a Forest Lying in Transition Zone between Lower and Upper Himalayan Moist Temperate Forest*, Puja Publishers, New Delhi, 1982.

Tripathi, R. S. and Barik, S. K. : *National Biodiversity Strategy and Action Plan Report for Northeast India*, Ministry of Environment and Forests, New Delhi, 2003.

Watt, Sir George : *Indian Art at Delhi 1903*, Government Printing, Calcutta, 1903.

White, G. : *The Natural History and Antiquities of Seibome*, McMillan, London, 1789.

Whittaker, R.H. : *Communities and Ecosystems*, Mac Millan Publishing Co., New York, 1975.

Index

❑❑❑

www.ingramcontent.com/pod-product-compliance
Ingram Content Group UK Ltd.
Pitfield, Milton Keynes, MK11 3LW, UK
UKHW042016290726
14061UKWH00001BB/28

9 789388 31887